SO-ATA-172

Family Breakup

𝓥 𝓥

Understanding Marital Problems
and the Mediating
of Child Custody Decisions

Marilyn Little

FAMILY
BREAKUP

𝓏 𝓏

Jossey-Bass Publishers
San Francisco • Washington • London • 1982

FAMILY BREAKUP
Understanding Marital Problems and the Mediating
of Child Custody Decisions
        by Marilyn Little

Copyright © 1982 by: Jossey-Bass Inc., Publishers
                     433 California Street
                     San Francisco, California 94104
                           &
                     Jossey-Bass Limited
                     28 Banner Street
                     London EC1Y 8QE

Library of Congress Cataloging in Publication Data

Little, Marilyn.
        Family breakup.

        Includes bibliographical references and index.
        1. Divorce—United States—Case studies.
2. Marriage—United States—Case studies.
3. Child custody—History. 4. Child custody—
United States—Case studies. 5. Children of
divorced parents—United States—Case studies.
I. Title.
HQ834.L7   1982   306.8'9   82-48068
ISBN 0-87589-552-2

Manufactured in the United States of America

The paper in this book meets the guidelines for
permanence and durability of the Committee on
Production Guidelines for Book Longevity of the
Council on Library Resources.

JACKET DESIGN BY WILLI BAUM

FIRST EDITION

Code 8243

The Jossey-Bass
Social and Behavioral Science Series

To Kris, Paul, Ted, and Jon Little

Preface

⅛ ⅛

This book is a study of how families approach separation and cope with divorce. It analyzes divorce and child custody decisions in terms of family bonds—the bonds between parent and child, husband and wife. Bonds are the ties of emotional affection, attachment, and loyalty that unite individuals within a family unit. Divorce implies a rearrangement of family bonds and raises questions not only of how emotional bonds can be maintained but also of actual physical location of family members—of who will live with whom. Physical custody of children, while it is a very important issue, is, in a sense, only a surface manifestation of the deeper threat divorce poses to maintenance of the parent-child bond. Divorce thus challenges the meaning of family ties and forces family members to appraise their relationships.

While many research studies have examined family formation, until recently little research focused on the divorcing family. Early studies of dissolution investigated the causes of divorce; research in the seventies dealt almost exclusively with
consequences of divorce for children and adults. Virtually no
research has focused on the *processes* by which family bonds
shift and deteriorate.

In examining patterns of separation and child custody decisions, this book contributes to several areas of family study. It
illuminates legal issues concerning child custody, an increasingly
important area of concern to professionals working with families. It presents graphic examples of negotiations and interaction, thus adding substance and vitality to descriptions of marital politics. It includes detailed family histories that give the
reader descriptive facts as well as theoretical insights; among
other things, these histories challenge popular stereotypes of
"unfit" or "selfish" women who lose or voluntarily relinquish
custody of their children. The book shows how couples' public
and private roles are integrated and interrelated—how, for example, the wife's return to work or the husband's unemployment can
trigger a shift in power in a marriage. In addition, the research
described here suggests that marital power is not limited to the
husband and wife. Ultimately the politics of the marriage involve the parent-child bonds and the roles children assume within the family. Finally, *Family Breakup* explores an overlooked
area of the family life cycle—the rearrangement and dissolution
of emotional bonds. By examining the diverse paths families
take as they move toward separation, this book clarifies the
variety of consequences experienced by divorcing couples and
their children.

Chapter One outlines briefly the legal and social history
of child custody and shows how social customs and attitudes
have changed from the time of the Romans to our modern society. It is a common assumption that mothers have always been
granted custody of their children and that the trend toward father custody is a new development in family history. This, however, is not the case. Until the beginning of the twentieth century, men were routinely awarded custody.

Chapter Two introduces forty divorcing couples and describes these men's and women's feelings about their jobs, marriages, and children. The three problems found most frequently among these families are discussed: work within and outside the home, the sexual relationship, and planning for and raising children. Since these couples are recently divorced, they are still struggling with intense emotional moods ranging from feelings of disappointment and failure to moments of acceptance and understanding. This chapter portrays their efforts to assimilate and cope with a poignant event in their lives.

Chapters Three, Four, and Five describe in detail six distinct marital patterns found among the forty families I studied. These patterns represent different interactive styles; they derive from daily behaviors that, over the years, develop into patterns and eventually shape the family's behavior at the time of separation. Whatever the family's pattern, it is actually created by the husband, wife, and child or children. It is manifested not only in the way they live together as a family but in the way they separate. Ultimately these patterns affect the decisions families make about custody of the children.

Chapter Six shows how the parents' relationship affects the children and what impact they, in turn, can have on the evolving marriage. The active roles children assume in the family can be categorized as "stabilizer," "competitor," "hostage," "caretaker," or "obstacle."

Chapter Seven contains a theoretical analysis of issues examined in this study. It describes how marriage, as an interactive process, is shaped by three important, closely related elements: power, status, and love. Changes in all three elements occur as couples "fall out of love" during the marriage. This chapter describes how the ideology of romantic love may conceal, for a while, the impact of changes in power and status because romantic love encourages maintenance of intense bonds that can be sustained only through idealization and denial of reality. An idealized relationship, however, soon becomes devoid of real intimacy.

Chapter Eight discusses the implications of this book for professionals who work with families. It addresses two major questions. First, to what extent can the information gleaned from these forty families contribute to our understanding of other families? A review of research by other social scientists suggests the marital and parenting experiences of these forty families are similar to the experiences of many families in our society. Insights from these men's and women's experiences may be useful in therapeutic work with other families, particularly when their interactive patterns are destructive.

Second, this chapter suggests ways in which professionals can assist families who contest custody in the courts. Issues pertinent to professionals working with these families include the role of the mental health professional in the legal process; the usefulness of nontraditional forms of conflict resolution, such as mediation and court investigation; the impact of politics on the legal process; and procedures to safeguard parents and children from family political maneuvering. A greater understanding of these issues will contribute to the professional's increased effectiveness in working with the families.

The primary audiences to whom this book is addressed are professionals who work with divorcing families: lawyers, social workers, psychologists, family therapists, and court counsellors and mediators. The analysis of children's roles within the context of marital patterns may provoke useful dialogue among social workers and family therapists who frequently work with children in separating families. Lawyers may gain new perspectives on family processes preceding divorce. The book may be particularly helpful to an emerging professional group: court counsellors and family mediators. The analysis of family patterns and children's roles will be of special value to these practitioners who work directly with families in the resolution of custody disputes.

A second audience consists of those professionals who are interested in theoretical issues as well as the substantive issues of divorce and custody. The development of patterns of power and negotiation and the maintenance and dissolution of family bonds are important to those who study the family, particularly in the disciplines of psychology, sociology, and social work.

Oakland, California   Marilyn Little
September 1982

Contents

𝒱 𝒱

    Contemporary Marriages   96

6. Children's Roles in Family Politics   115

7. The Impact of Divorce on Children   148

8. Helping Parents and Children Through
    Crisis and Divorce   169

    Appendix: Research Notes   207

    References   217

    Index   227

Family
Breakup

*Understanding Marital Problems
and the Mediating
of Child Custody Decisions*

1

𝔑 𝔑

Changes
in Laws and Customs
Regarding Child Custody

𝒴 𝒴

As divorce rates continue to escalate, child custody will become an increasingly important issue confronting many families. Current estimates indicate that by 1990 approximately one third of the children will experience a parental divorce before they reach the age of eighteen (Glick, 1979). Families must negotiate caretaking arrangements for these children. In the past, separating families were guided in their decisions by laws that stated a very clear preference for one parent. Historically, the father was favored; in more recent years the mother has been regarded as the primary parent. Many state laws now forbid preference on the basis of sex (Brown, Freedman, Katz, and Price, 1977). Thus, mothers can no longer assume they will automatically receive custody simply because they are women.

Emphasis on the legal aspects of determining child custody, however, overlooks a very important and intriguing fact: in over 90 percent of divorce cases, the family determines who will have custody of the child before the legal process is initiated (Weiss, 1976). Thus, it is the family, and more particularly, the husband and wife, who make these decisions.

This book examines the family's approach to separation: How do families divide themselves? How do a husband and wife make decisions about custody? To what extent do children become involved in this issue? Since the great majority of cases are not contested, the implication is that one parent willingly relinquishes the custodial role to the other parent. In a culture that has placed so much emphasis on the woman's role as mother, why and how do women arrive at a point at which they are willing to voluntarily leave their children with the father? Why do fathers seek this responsibility?

In the absence of knowledge based on systematic study, a folklore has emerged to explain family situations that deviate from the norm of mother custody. One stereotype developed from the legal custom of withholding custody from mothers who were deemed "unfit" to care for their children. Even though laws have changed and sex roles have become less rigid, the myth lingers. Mothers who lose custody of their children must be unfit parents.

A new stereotype has emerged in recent years. This image has arisen from changing sex roles for men and women. It reflects the fear and suspicion that once women become liberated from their traditional roles, they will abandon their parenting role. According to this myth, mothers leave because they have been exposed to feminist teachings and are no longer interested in parenting.

This book is based on the lives of real men and women. Their life experiences challenge and refute the simplicity of stereotypical explanations of divorce and custody and illustrate the complexity of this life event. First, their experiences demonstrate the importance of family history. Divorce is not an isolated event; decisions made in this period must be examined within the context of family history. Second, their accounts testify to the complexity of family relationships. Custody decisions are affected by the husband/wife relationship as well as by the parent/child relationship. Third, a careful analysis of their reports suggests that power is a key component of family interaction and is a critical factor in developing any theoretical explanation of family separation.

Experiences recounted in this book will illustrate very clearly that the decisions made at the time of the divorce are rooted in family history. First, the actions men and women take toward each other and their children at the time of divorce are not new, unpredicted actions; rather, they are the end points in a long line of familiar, established behaviors. The pain of separation simply intensifies and makes more visible old family rules and behaviors. Embedded within the family history, the choices regarding child custody are extensions of these old family rules.

Second, decisions made by these families reflect the complexity of family bonds. Unlike the stereotypes that focus attention on only one member of the family—the woman—these men's and women's experiences testify to the interrelatedness of family members. Custody arrangements are not based on one parent's superior or inferior functioning, nor do they simply reflect the dyadic relationship of mother and child. The child lives within a context of complex family relationships. The husband/ wife relationship is of particular importance to children. The marital interaction influences each parent's response to the child and creates an ambience within the home. The child's behavior, in turn, has a profound impact on the marriage. At the time of divorce, custodial arrangements reflect this complex web of family relationships, a web that, incidentally, is only partly visible to persons outside the family.

Third, power exercised by individual members affects family decisions. The experiences of these men and women suggest, however, that power is not a static attribute possessed by each individual. It may be described more aptly as a process in which family members negotiate, maneuver, and make use of their resources to gain desired goals. To emphasize this concept of process rather than static attribution, the term *powering* will be used in this book to describe the attempts of men and women to control and shape their relationship. Each person's position within the family does not remain constant but shifts in response to changes in internal and external conditions. For example, the birth of a child, a woman's return to work, or a man's sudden unemployment may trigger a shift in relative bargaining positions. Powering, this dynamic movement within the family, shapes the way the family separates just as it affects the way they live together. An understanding of the politics of the family thus contributes to an increased understanding of their decisions on custody. When custody decisions are examined with an emphasis on continuity, complexity, and power, a more sophisticated awareness replaces the simple stereotypes.

Historical Perspectives on Child Custody

Although stereotypes do not contribute to a sophisticated understanding of family behaviors, they generally have some basis in historical events. Over the years, interpretation of these events becomes overly simplified. The old stereotype of "unfit" mothers losing custody emerged from a particular period of time when women were preferred as custodial parents. However, mothers enjoyed this preference for a relatively short time. Until the beginning of the twentieth century, fathers automatically received custody, unless they were deemed unfit guardians for the child. Their custodial rights were part of their rights and responsibilities as heads of the household, a legal right extending back in history to Roman law. A brief review of this historical evolution of custodial rights places in perspective our current social and legal positions on custody.

Patria Potestas: The Father's Right. In Roman law, *patria potestas* referred to paternal authority and power. This doctrine gave the father the power of life and death over his children. In a later period of history it limited his control to property (Black, 1951). This doctrine also gave the father absolute right over custody, a power that extended even beyond his death. If he appointed a guardian before his death, the guardian rather than the mother had custody of the children upon his death. Moreover, if the mother remarried after his death, she might lose custody of the children to a third party. Roman law enjoined the children to show due reverence and respect to their mother, but beyond that she had no rights (Schouler and Blakemore, 1921, p. 740).

The concept of the father's absolute right was carried over into English common law but was relaxed a bit by a statute known as Justice Talfourd's Act in 1839. According to this act, the father's rights remained predominant but only if he was maintaining his marital obligations toward his wife. For the first time, also, the law indicated that the father should pay attention to the interests of his children (Schouler and Blakemore, 1921, p. 742).

Although the father's right continued into American law, some commentators argue that it was not as strictly adhered to as it had been in common law (Brown, 1927; Madden, 1931; Schouler and Blakemore, 1921). However, writing in the early part of the twentieth century, legal commentators said that if all other things were equal, the father would still be preferred as the custodial parent. In a divorce the wife might petition for custody, but the burden of proof would be on her to establish the father's unfitness (Schouler and Blakemore, 1921, p. 749). If the father and mother were equally entitled to custody, the father could also take the child peaceably from the mother without committing the crime of kidnaping. Commentators do not indicate whether the wife had the same right to take the child from the father without being charged with kidnaping. Since the father had preference, it probably was difficult for the woman to take her child forcibly.

Services and Support: Principle of Reciprocity. The father's rights over his children were established before the child's corresponding rights for protection and support. The notion that children have rights is, legally speaking, a recent development. Early legal formulations of the father's rights over his children protected his property rights; the children were regarded as his chattel (Jacobs and Goebel, 1962). The concept of the father's responsibility for the child and the child's rights developed gradually. At first it was assumed that fathers were guided by "natural" or "moral" laws in caring for their chil-

dren. These natural constraints made protective laws unneces-
sary. Blackstone, for example, argued that natural forces were
"working so strongly as to need rather a check than a spur"
(quoted in Schouler and Blakemore, 1921). Other legal commentators also stated: "It is to the credit of our civilization that
the natural duty of protection is rather permitted than enjoined
by any municipal laws" (quoted in Schouler and Blakemore,
1921, p. 773).

The state's right to determine and enforce paternal responsibility evolved very slowly. In the nineteenth century
courts gained jurisdiction over this relationship through the application of the concept of *parens patriae*. This doctrine gives
the state a sovereign power of guardianship over persons who
are disabled, are insane, or are incompetent (Black, 1951, p.
1269). In 1839, through Justice Talfourd's Act, the concept
of *parens patriae* was extended to include infants, and the
courts were given authority to award custody of children under
the age of seven. By the end of the nineteenth century, the laws
were changed to give courts jurisdiction over all minors (Foster
and Freed, 1964, Part I; Madden, 1931).

According to a principle of reciprocity, the courts believed that the father, who supported the child, was also entitled to the child's services. These services included labor within the home and wages from outside employment. Women,
because they did not support their children, were not entitled
to these services. If the family divorced, the husband, it was argued, should continue to enjoy the services of his children, since
he continued to be obligated for their support. Numerous cases
debated around the turn of the century reveal the complications
involved in attempting to maintain the link between support
and services. Some courts declared that the father did not need
to support the child if the mother had custody and received the
benefits of the child's labor; other courts stated that the father
must continue to provide support but only if he had been guilty
of misconduct during the marriage; others, in more complicated
motions, said the father was still entitled to services because of
his obligation to provide legal support, even if the mother had
custody (*Hall* v. *Green,* 1895; *Ross* v. *Richardson,* 1928; *Fulton*
v. *Fulton,* 1895; *Keller* v. *City of St. Louis,* 1899).

One legal scholar who reviewed the complicated connection of responsibilities and privileges recommended discarding the concept of reciprocity. He recommended that the duty of support should be determined independently of any formula of reciprocity ("Notes," *Harvard Law Review,* 1928). Gradually over a period of time the courts dropped their concern for services and made recommendations on support only.

Maternal Preference: The Doctrine of Tender Years. Although the father was still regarded as the preferred parent through the first two decades of the twentieth century, some courts and judges were beginning to reverse their preferences. As early as 1872, the U.S. Supreme Court ruled in one case that the mother was the more important parent. The court proposed that a particular family order was divinely decreed: "The constitution of the family organization, which is founded in the Divine ordinance, as well as in the nature of things, indicates the domestic sphere as that which properly belongs in the domain and functions of womanhood . . . The paramount destiny and mission of women are to fulfil the noble and benign offices of wife and mother. This is the law of the creator" (opinion in *Bradwell* v. *Illinois,* 83 U.S. 130, 141, 1872, quoted in Tritico, 1974, p. 882).

In determination of custody, the courts began to consider such factors as age, sex, and health of the child. If the child was very young, the courts perceived the mother as the more appropriate parent. The rather vague phrase *tender years* began to appear in several court opinions: "For a boy of such tender years nothing can be an adequate substitute for mother love—for that constant ministration required during the period of nurture that only a mother can give because in her alone is duty swallowed up in desire; in her alone is service expressed in terms of love. She alone has the patience and sympathy required to mold and soothe the infant mind in its adjustment to its environment" (*Jenkins* v. *Jenkins,* 173 Wisconsin, 1921, quoted in Weiss, 1976, p. 15).

Kram and Frank (1976) indicate that in one of the first cases in the state of New York that ruled in favor of the mother, the judge made his decision on the basis of the child's age: "The child at tender age is entitled to have such care, love, and discipline as only a good and devoted mother can usually give. This should continue from intimate association until the infancy grows into childhood" (*Ullman* v. *Ullman,* 151 App. Div. 415, 135 NYS 1080, 1082, 2nd Dept., quoted in Kram and Frank, 1976, p. 14).

Tender years was never defined. While it most certainly included children to the age of seven, it may also have included preadolescent children (Weiss, 1976). Preference was also given to mothers if the child was female or in "delicate condition" (Madden, 1931; Brown, 1927).

After 1927 the doctrine of maternal preference expanded quickly. Some states explicitly granted preference to the mother if the child was of "tender years"; others did not state this preference in their statutes but followed it in practice (Weiss, 1976). In 1976 Freed and Foster claimed that this presumption was so well established that in over 90 percent of the contested custody cases, courts ruled in favor of the mother. Kram and Frank also concluded that in spite of isolated cases reversing this presumption, the doctrine of "tender years" was currently alive and well in the courts around the country in the mid-seventies. This doctrine may wane in the eighties as more attention is given to the father's position in the family.

The Unfit Parent. The courts have at many times overruled the prevailing assumptions and reversed the usual preferences. This has generally been done only if the parent normally assumed to have custodial rights has been judged "unfit." Under the common law of England it was very difficult, almost impossible, to demonstrate the unfitness of the father. Only if the courts judged that the misbehavior could cause moral or physical damage were they willing to remove the child from the father. Atheism, blasphemy, irreligion, and poisoning the child's mind with religious opinions "dangerous to society" were the most shameful offenses prompting courts to take children from the father. In one of the more celebrated cases, the poet Shelley lost his children because of his atheistic beliefs (*Shelley* v. *Westbrooke,* Jacob 266, 37 Eng. Rep. 850, Ch. 1817, cited by Foster and Freed, 1964, Part I). Poverty or adultery was not sufficient to deprive the father of his children.

Similar judgments were, of course, applied to women also. In 1879 Mrs. Besant lost custody of her son and daughter in spite of a separation deed granting her custody. She refused to give her children religious education and was convicted of obscene libel for publishing a book on birth control. The court reasoned that these actions would cut the mother and daughter off from other women (Foster and Freed, 1964, Part I, pp. 424-425).

Over the years the courts eventually included other factors in determining a parent's fitness: drunkenness, cruelty, violence, desertion, and mental illness. Violence, when directed toward the spouse and not directly toward the child, may not be sufficient to determine a parent unfit (*Mills* v. *Mills,* 218 Ga. 686, 130 S.E. 2nd 221, 1963, quoted in Foster and Freed, 1964). A double standard has existed on adultery. A woman's adulterous behavior has often been regarded as sufficient proof of immorality, but a man's adultery has not been regarded as a sufficiently serious factor to deprive him of custody (Foster and Freed, 1964, Part I, p. 431).

The Best Interests of the Child. In awarding custody, parental rights have dominated decision making. For many years the child as property belonged to the father. Then the mother was deemed the natural parent. Gradually it was recognized that society's best interests were promoted by making sure children were reared in the best possible manner to assure their effectiveness as adult citizens. The "best interests of the child" became a more dominant concern in awarding custody. In 1963 the Family Law Section of the American Bar Association stated that "custody *shall* be awarded . . . according to the best interests of the child" (Benedek and Benedek, 1972, p. 826; emphasis by Benedek and Benedek). The Revised Uniform Marriage and Divorce Act, written as a model for state legislation, stipulates that the court "shall determine custody in accordance with the best interests of the child" (Shepherd, 1974, p. 172).

As laws change and place more emphasis on the child's well-being, it will be increasingly difficult for courts to award custody on the basis of sex of parent. If the Equal Rights Amendment ever passes, it will be illegal to base custody deci-

sions on sex. Courts may consider such factors as parental life-
style, arrangements for care of child, and relationship with the
child. However, all issues must be shown to be related to the
child's welfare and must be applied across the board to parents
of both sexes (Brown, Freedman, Katz, and Price, 1977). Undoubtedly, for families of the future, custody will be an open
issue, one not easily resolved by an appeal to fixed social customs and laws.

Research Questions and Methods

When laws and social customs no longer regulate custody
of children following a divorce, what factors do affect the placement of children? Early in this study, I decided there were two
sets, or levels, of questions, each requiring a different methodo-
logical approach. One set of questions addressed larger issues and
focused on the relations of demographic variables to custodial
arrangements. How, for example, do number, age, and sex of
children affect determination of child custody? Does social class
influence the family's arrangements at the time of divorce?

To address these questions, I collected data from court
records for 600 families. These families were randomly selected
from all divorce cases filed in an urban county in Northern California between September 1976 and December 1977. Results of
the analysis of these data are reported elsewhere (Little, 1980).

The second set of questions focused on internal relationships within the family. What prompts women to leave their
families? Why do some fathers seek custody, while others do
not? How do couples negotiate an agreement on custody? Sta-
tistical data from court records could not, of course, answer
these questions. To examine family interactions, I interviewed
forty men and women. These respondents were selected from
the larger sample of 600 families. Since my sample was small, I
decided to control for class and selected only those families in
which the husband had a professional or white-collar position.
In each family I chose either the husband or wife for interview.
The final sample contained an equal number of men and wom-
en from mother- and father-custody families: ten men and ten

women from twenty father-custody families and ten men and ten women from twenty mother-custody families.

The forty interviewed families were evenly distributed in the family life cycle, as indicated by age of the oldest child. In approximately one third of these families, the oldest child was either preschool, school age, or teenage. The parents, however, were not young. Over half the men (twenty-three) and almost half the women (nineteen) were thirty-six or older. Half the marriages were also eleven years or longer in duration, with the longest marriage twenty-seven years.

Men were employed in a wide variety of professional and white-collar positions, including engineering, law, medicine, management, sales, and teaching in high school and college. Very few women were employed in the professions. Aside from three college professors, one engineer, and four elementary school teachers, most women worked as clerks, secretaries, bookkeepers, and managers of small offices. A small handful were in health-related fields or in real estate or accounting.

I used a structured interview schedule that included questions about marital life, divorce, and custody. Interviews were extensive and lasted three hours or more. A few lengthy interviews were completed in two sessions. All interviews were taped and transcribed. Names were, of course, changed to pseudonyms to protect each person's identity.

Interviews were all divided into segments and each segment analyzed for husband/wife, parent/child behaviors. Early in the analysis, I listed all behaviors described by men and women. An extensive list of behaviors included everything from praising and persuading to demanding, threatening, and beating. As I proceeded to identify these behaviors, I noted that they could be grouped into three general categories: behaviors that moved the husband and wife *away from* each other (Avoidance), *against* each other (Attack), or *toward* each other (Appeal). Appeal behaviors could be further subdivided into Subordinate and Superordinate. Subordinate Appeal behaviors—asking, supplicating, crying—revealed the person's lower status. The Superordinate Appeal behaviors, in contrast, implied that the person made demands from a position of greater power or authority. Assuming superiority, this person expected the mate to comply with demands.

Eventually I was able to construct an outline of behaviors, ranging from the more subtle to the more visible, in each of these four categories (see Research Notes in the Appendix). Using this guide, I compared families and grouped those together that were most similar in interactive style. In this way, I identified six patterns of family interaction: Fragile Bond, Fractured Family, Doll's House, Stalemate, Perfect Model, and Unformed Family.

Preview of Family Patterns

In two of the six family patterns, couples followed fairly traditional roles. In Fragile Bond and Fractured Families, women spent most of their time and energy in the home caring for children, while men developed careers. *Fragile Bond* marriages were quiet marriages, as both husbands and wives withdrew and moved away from each other when they encountered problems. Men and women in these six marriages maintained a deceptive tranquility by avoiding confrontation on troublesome issues. Over the years, they drifted apart emotionally but clung to the shell of their marriage. One day, quite suddenly, the marriage ended when one partner simply walked away. The abrupt ending shocked the spouse left in the home.

Although the men and women in the ten *Fractured Families* also followed traditional roles, they developed a very different pattern of interaction. Within the Fractured Families, men avoided their wives and were verbally and sometimes physically abusive to them. Women attempted to gain support for themselves through emotional appeals, but as they increased their appeals, men became more withdrawn and abusive. Both women and children in these families eventually had problems requiring professional attention. Several children had emotional and learning problems; five of the ten wives received treatment for problems such as drug and alcohol addiction and mental health problems. Within these homes, relationships were fractured not by the divorce itself but by the destructive behaviors exhibited in daily living.

In the eight *Doll's House Marriages,* men and women were emotionally committed to their marriage and valued family life. In the early stages of the marriage, men dominated through subtle behaviors of rewarding, persuading, demanding, and devaluing. At some point in the marriage, however—usually following the woman's return to work or entry into therapy—women changed their behavior patterns and became more assertive. In some families roles changed further as women became increasingly successful in their careers and men had trouble with employment. Like Nora in Ibsen's play *A Doll's House,* these women began to perceive their marriage as a stifling prison. They eventually decided to leave the marriage.

In the four *Stalemate Marriages,* the men characteristically avoided strong emotional confrontations and withdrew from their families. Women moved aggressively against this withdrawal by demanding, pleading, criticizing, and finally threatening their husbands. These movements resulted in a deadlocked position, similar to a stalemate position in chess. In this condition, neither partner can move, and the game ends in a draw. When these couples reached a stalemate position, the women, who appeared much more dissatisfied with the unproductive communication patterns, left the home.

Men and women in the eight *Perfect Model Marriages* were young, well educated, and successful in their professions. Although these marriages appeared more egalitarian than others, discounting, dismissing, and criticizing suggested a subtle, sophisticated form of male dominance. In addition, illusions of a Perfect Model of marriage enabled these men and women to maintain emotional distance in their relationship. In seven of these eight families, the men moved away from the home as they became restless and dissatisfied with their wives.

The three young *Unformed Families* had been together only three years when they separated. Women appeared unready for marriage and had some difficulty forming bonds with their husbands and children. These brief marriages were characterized by women's withdrawal and flight from the home and men's confusion and complaints about their wives' coldness and avoidance of intimacy. When these women left their families, men felt confused and angry with the women for abandoning their roles as mothers and wives.

As families lived together, parenting patterns developed in conjunction with the marital patterns. Divorcing families revealed five types of parenting patterns: *Maternal, Shared, Uncommitted, Paternal,* and *Split.* Children also assumed a role in the family drama, as *Stabilizer, Competitor, Hostage, Caretaker,* or *Obstacle.* The parenting patterns and children's roles were shaped and influenced by four major factors: (1) marital politics, (2) the husband's and wife's patterns of employment and unemployment, (3) parental stress, as indicated by failure in family planning and conflict in child rearing, and (4) sex and age of the children.

In Fragile Bond families, women were regarded as the primary parents. Children were *Stabilizers*; they added meaning to life. Family activities centered on the children, and their presence contributed to the woman's sense of satisfaction and accomplishment. Some men resented the children's predominant position and felt the children were *Competitors* for attention from the wife. For other men, the children were Stabilizers; like their wives, they felt the children added meaning and enjoyment to life. Traditional roles and the wives' prominence in parenting characterized these families in a *Maternal Parenting* pattern. At the time of divorce both men and women assumed the women would retain custody of the children.

The *Shared* and *Uncommitted Parenting* patterns differed greatly from each other. In the *Shared* pattern, both parents retained a warm, close relationship with the child before and after the divorce. For both parents the child acted as a *Stabilizer*; that is, children were central to these people's lives. Both parents felt it was critically important to maintain contact with the children after divorce, regardless of which parent had physical custody. Most of the parents in this Shared Parenting pattern were from Perfect Model marriages. Women generally had careers, and men had shared more responsibility for children throughout the family's history. The women's employment, a more egalitarian relationship, and a low degree of stress in childbearing and child rearing contributed to these couples' ability to share responsibility for the children after divorce.

Conversely, coercive, punitive power exercised within the marriage, the wife's dependent status, and high parental stress all contributed to unusually high family tensions in the Fractured Families. Children, depending on their age and sex, played either a Hostage or Caretaker role in these families. In some families, teenage children served as *Hostages* or pawns as they were used by each parent to retaliate against the mate. Failure in family planning and daily struggles in raising several closely spaced children diminished parental effectiveness. Years of stressful marital conflict further eroded the couple's ability to function as caring, competent parents. By the time of divorce, these men and women were often in an *Uncommitted Parenting* pattern. They were able to give only a minimum amount of attention to their parenting responsibilities. Frequently the couple's hostilities extended beyond the divorce, and children continued in a Hostage role.

In other Fractured Families, children were seduced into playing the role of *Caretaker* for the parent cast as "loser" in the marital battle. Roles were reversed as the child attempted to nurture and care for the victimized parent. In three Doll's House Marriages, children were also lured into this role of Caretaker. In the three Doll's House and the three Fractured Families in which the child assumed this role, the important element was the child's perception of the parents' marriage. The children in these homes perceived one parent as the loser. A noticeable imbalance in power in the husband/wife relationship impelled the child into a protective alignment with the "losing" parent. Sadly for the children, this sometimes meant they moved away from the more effective and capable parent. These families were in a *Split Parenting* pattern; the split between the husband and wife was reflected in a split within children who loved both parents but felt compelled to support one over the other.

The fifth pattern, *Paternal Parenting,* resembled the Maternal Parenting pattern; one parent—in this case, the father—assumed a primary role with the children. For these men, the children were *Stabilizers* who added to the structure and meaning of life. Their wives did not share this feeling. Women in these homes had moved away from parenting. In fact, for some, children had become *Obstacles* to the development of their own

lives. This parenting pattern did not match well with any particular marital pattern. Three of the four Stalemate Marriages and
seven families from other marital patterns were included in the
Paternal Parenting group. Paternal Parenting is, thus, less connected to a particular type of husband/wife relationship; what
these families did share was a similar response among women.
These women rejected marital and parenting roles that they felt
were confining and rigid.

Family life is complex, and the correlations between
marital and parenting patterns are far from perfect. It is clear,
however, that marital politics affects parenting. Among these
families, the husband/wife relationship shaped the parent/child
relationship and the child's role in the family. Various configura-
tions of marital powering affected the family's evolution and
the paths they followed toward separation.

2

Explaining Marital Failure:
Private Disclosures
and Public Accounts

The forty men and women in this study did not share similar perceptions about the problems within their marriages, but they agreed on the ideals they cherished for that relationship. They valued marriage for the intimacy and companionship it could provide and wanted partners capable of understanding, listening, and showing affection. They also valued partners who could share parenting and care for the children's needs.

They shared, too, a sense of their own failure and a bitter disappointment in their partner's failure to meet their expectations. As they assessed their own and their spouse's behavior in the marriage, they were most unhappy with performance in those areas that were most important to them. They were bitterly disappointed and angry with their partner's failure to meet their needs and a little chagrined and defensive about their own failure. Their struggle to understand and accept these failures was painful; moments of acceptance and insight were interwoven with moments of denial and anger. The fluctuating emotional moods contributed to ever-changing definitions of their situation, as they continued to assess and reassess their own and their spouse's behaviors.

The areas of family life in which they most frequently expressed a keen disappointment included the division of work within and outside the home, the sexual relationship, and childbearing and child rearing. They were most ambivalent about their experiences with employment and work within the home. Men, particularly, sensed that their stated beliefs did not always match their behaviors. They recognized that they approved of their wives' employment, but they also resented the wife's absence from home. They recognized her right to ask for more help in the home but also admitted to feeling "messed up" and weak if they capitulated to these demands. Women wanted their husbands to be successful but resented the commitment that success demanded. They felt deprived of their husband's attention and feared that his emotional commitment to work was greater than his commitment to the marital relationship and to the family.

Children presented another ambiguity for these families. Virtually all men and women wanted children; only two or three respondents knew from the beginning that they did not want children. Men and women alike assumed it was a natural part of marriage; for many, it was not even an issue for discussion. But the conception of children, their arrival, and their training presented unanticipated problems. For women the parenting experience was a very powerful experience. They were more affected by the pregnancy period and most intensively affected by the period immediately following the birth of the first child. Some were surprised and confused by the intensity of negative feelings. They acknowledged their ambivalence about raising children and recognized the existence of strong negative and positive emotional currents between them and the children. Men generally reported a less intense emotional response to the birth of the child and perceived the child-rearing process as more rational and manageable.

Although couples often differed in their ideas about the right approach to disciplining children, they less frequently criticized each other's nurturance of the child. Very few men and women judged their spouse inadequate in emotionally caring for the child.

Both men and women recognized that children had a powerful impact on the marriage. Their arrival, whether planned or not, changed the relationship.

Images and Realities

Men and women shared some common hopes for marriage and family life. When the respondents were given a list of twelve possible characteristics of the ideal marital partner and were asked to rank these in desirability, they responded very similarly (Tables 1 through 4). Men and women agreed that, ideally, the most important characteristic for either a husband or a wife is the ability to be a companion, to share interests and enjoy life with the partner. They valued the closeness of the marital relationship and the intimate sharing of feelings and thoughts; they also wanted a partner who would listen to them and encourage them. And they would like a partner who is sexually attractive. These qualities of personal responsiveness were among the most important characteristics and were the most desired by both men and women.

The second cluster of ideal characteristics focused on the mate as a parent. Men and women want a mate who is able to care for the children's physical and emotional needs. They want a mate who can be a model for the child, who possesses the type of character and personality a child can identify with and imitate.

A third cluster of characteristics included less personal contributions to the functioning of the home: working and providing for the family financially, managing the family income and finances, and working within the home to make it more attractive. These activities, important as they may be to the func-

Table 1. Role Characteristics of Ideal Husband, and Husband's
Performance in These Roles, as Judged by Women (*N* = 20).

Characteristic of Ideal Mate	Husband's Performance in Role		Characteristic
Ranking	Rank of Rating	Mean Rating[a]	
1st	6th	3.20	He is a companion to his wife, sharing interests, enjoying life with her.
2nd	9th	3.40	He listens to his wife, encourages and comforts her.
3rd	10th	3.40	He shares his inner feelings, thoughts, fears, and dreams with his wife.
4th	3rd	2.90	He is an attractive sexual partner to his wife.
5th	1st	1.85	He works and contributes to the family financially.
6th	2nd	2.45	He cares for the children's physical and emotional needs.
7th	4th	3.05	He serves as a model of men for the children.
8th	11th	3.70	He helps manage the family income and finances.
9th	5th	3.05	He does his work around the house and puts energy into making it an attractive house.
10th	12th	4.05	He practices the family religion and philosophy.
11th	7th	3.25	He decides when the family is still divided after discussing something.
12th	8th	3.25	He represents the family socially in the community.

[a]Women rated husband's performance as follows: (1) excellent performance, (2) above average, (3) about average, (4) below average, (5) never displayed this characteristic.

tioning of the home, were ranked as considerably less important than the personal responses of a caring mate and parent.

The reality of married life did not live up to the respondents' hopes and images. When the men and women were asked to rate their own performance and that of their spouse in each

Table 2. Role Characteristics of Ideal Husband, and Their Own
Performance in These Roles, as Judged by Men (N = 19).

Characteristic of Ideal Husband	Own Performance in Role		Characteristic
Ranking	Rank of Rating	Mean Rating[a]	Characteristic
1st	9th	3.00	He is a companion to his wife, sharing interests, enjoying life with her.
2nd	10th	3.11	He shares his inner feelings, thoughts, fears, and dreams with his wife.
3rd	7th	2.84	He listens to his wife, encourages and comforts her.
4th	3rd	2.05	He cares for the children's physical and emotional needs.
5th	6th	2.74	He is an attractive sexual partner.
6th	1st	1.16	He works and contributes to the family financially.
7th	5th	2.11	He does his work around the house and puts energy into making it an attractive house.
8th	2nd	1.95	He serves as a model of men for the children.
9th	4th	2.05	He helps manage the family income and finances.
10th	11th	3.26	He practices the family religion or philosophy.
11th	8th	2.89	He decides when the family is still divided after discussing something.
12th	12th	3.47	He represents the family socially in the community.

[a]Men rated their performance as follows: (1) excellent performance, (2) above average, (3) about average, (4) below average, (5) never displayed this characteristic.

of these areas, it became quite clear that respondents felt both they and their spouses had failed within the marriage. They rated performance in those areas most important to them as lowest. For example, men named companionship as the most important characteristic of the ideal mate; their rating of their own performance as companions to their wives was very low,

Table 3. Role Characteristics of Ideal Wife, and Wife's Performance
in These Roles, as Judged by Men (*N* = 19).

Characteristic of Ideal Mate	Wife's Performance in Role		
Ranking	Rank of Rating	Mean Rating[a]	Characteristic
1st	12th	3.58	She is a companion to her husband, sharing interests, enjoying life with him.
2nd	10th	2.75	She shares her inner feelings, thoughts, fears, and dreams with her husband.
3rd	1st	2.26	She cares for the children's physical and emotional needs.
4th	5th	2.95	She is an attractive sexual partner.
5th	8th	2.20	She listens to her husband, encourages and comforts him.
6th	2nd	2.58	She does her work around the house and puts energy into making it an attractive house.
7th	3rd	1.65	She helps manage the family income and finances.
8th	4th	2.90	She serves as a model of women for the children.
9th	10th	3.21	She works and contributes to the family financially.
10th	6th	3.11	She practices the family religion or philosophy.
11th	10th	3.21	She decides when the family is still divided after discussing something.
12th	7th	3.11	She represents the family socially in the community.

[a]Men rated wife's performance as follows: (1) excellent performance, (2) above average, (3) about average, (4) below average, (5) never displayed this characteristic.

lower than the ratings they gave themselves in eight other areas. Similarly, their performance on the second-most-valued behavior, intimate sharing, was the third-lowest rating they gave themselves (Table 2).

Their rating of their wives' performance was even lower; they judged that their wives performed the most poorly (twelfth)

Table 4. Role Characteristics of Ideal Wife, and Their Own Performance in These Roles, as Judged by Women (N = 20).

Characteristic of Ideal Wife	Own Performance in Role		Characteristic
Ranking	Rank of Rating	Mean Rating[a]	Characteristic
1st	7th	2.30	She is a companion to her husband, sharing interests, enjoying life with him.
2nd	4th	2.20	She listens to her husband, encourages and comforts him.
3rd	2nd	1.70	She cares for the children's physical and emotional needs.
4th	10th	2.75	She shares her inner feelings, thoughts, fears, and dreams with her husband.
5th	8th	2.45	She is an attractive sexual partner to her husband.
6th	3rd	1.95	She serves as a model of women for the children.
7th	5th	2.25	She does her work around the house and puts energy into making it an attractive house.
8th	1st	1.65	She helps manage the family income and finances.
9th	12th	3.26	She practices the family religion or philosophy.
10th	6th	2.25	She works and contributes to the family financially.
11th	9th	2.65	She decides when the family is still divided after discussing something.
12th	11th	2.80	She represents the family socially in the community.

[a]Women rated their own performance as follows: (1) excellent performance, (2) above average, (3) about average, (4) below average, (5) never displayed this characteristic.

in the most important area, companionship, and almost as poorly (tenth) in the second behavior, intimate sharing (Table 3).

Women were similarly disappointed with their husbands' performance in these roles (Table 1). Ratings they gave their husbands on the three most important characteristics were in the middle or among the lowest of all their ratings (sixth, ninth, and tenth). Women rated themselves a little higher on marital interaction (Table 4). They felt they had been relatively good companions, who had listened to their husbands and encouraged them. They were more critical of themselves in their ability to share intimately and be an attractive sexual partner.

Men and women did not judge parenting functions to be as important as the more intimate marital responsibilities. However, they felt they and their spouses had done well in caring for the children and serving as models for them. Men and women alike rated themselves and their partners quite high on parenting.

Within the third cluster of characteristics, contributions to the functioning of the home, men and women gave themselves and their partners some fairly high ratings, with two exceptions: women felt their husbands had contributed to the family financially and had helped around the house, but they were very critical of their husbands for not helping manage the family income and finances. Men felt their wives had contributed to taking care of the home and had helped with managing the money, but they were critical of them for not contributing more to the family financially.

The largest disparities between the ideal and the reality are reflected within those behaviors representing the core of marital life: the intimate role of the husband and wife. Here both men and women feel their partners failed them. The men, particularly, also believe they did not live up to their own expectations in those areas. They feel the pain of not receiving what they hoped for in the marriage, but perhaps even more, they believe that in the most critical areas of the marriage, they failed.

Responses to these scales highlight two important issues within these families. First, both men and women value the husband/wife bonds. Next in significance and priority are the bonds with the children. They want partners who will first of all be loving mates and, second, caring parents.

Second, they are most disappointed in the failure of their marriages. They feel bitterly disappointed about their partner's failure to meet their personal needs. When the responses are examined more closely and ratings for their own behavior are compared with their ratings for their spouse's behavior, both men and women, as groups, give themselves higher ratings than they give their spouses in every area, with one exception. Women rate their husbands as higher in the area of working and contributing financially to the household, while men rate their wives as higher in their social contributions to the community. But in all other eleven areas of marital responsibility, both men and women generally felt they performed better than their spouses.

This keen sense of betrayal and bitter disappointment gives the interviews a note of defensiveness. These men and women are still in the midst of extricating themselves from marriages in which they were badly hurt. It is a time of bitterness and emotional distress, with perhaps only the beginning hints of self-appraisal.

In the interviews, these poignant notes of self-appraisal are interwoven with defensive accusations. Following a passage in which a respondent angrily criticizes the spouse, he or she may describe in considerable detail some painfully acquired new insight. Newly divorced men and women are, thus, not rigidly consistent in their perceptions of their marriages. Rather, they vacillate in tone and mood as they struggle to include the old history and new insights into a new definition of their situation.

During the course of the interview, people talked about many areas of their married life. As they were given an opportunity to talk at length about these areas, it became quite obvious that in each marriage there were a number of issues causing considerable difficulty. These in-depth discussions revealed that the most problematic areas were the husband's and wife's employment and the division of work within the home, the sexual relationship, and childbearing and child rearing.

Work Within and Outside the Home

Both men and women talked about problems with employment outside the home and the division of work within the home. Over two thirds (women, 65 percent; men, 70 percent)

reported conflict over the issue of women's employment or unemployment. Almost that many (women, 65 percent; men, 60
percent) also felt the husbands' work created some conflict. In
discussing problems emanating from women's work, it was apparent that the reentry situation caused the most conflict for
families. For men, problems involved two very different kinds
of situations: the overcommitted worker and the underachieving worker.

The Reentry Worker. The most serious difficulties connected with women's employment arose in those families experiencing a reentry of the woman to employment after some
time at home with the children. Two other types of situations
seemed less troublesome. In twelve families, the wife remained
home after the children arrived and did not work until immediately preceding the divorce, when finances made it imperative
for her to work. In these families very little friction was created
by the woman's commitment to full-time housekeeping. While
seven of these twelve men apparently encouraged their wives to
work, the decisions to remain at home apparently did not cause
conflict.

In a second type of situation, women worked for the major portion of the marriage. Seven of these fifteen homes reported no problems with the woman's employment. In the remaining eight, the respondents indicated the wife's work was a
source of tension.

The most serious conflicts arose, however, in those homes
in which the wife returned to work after being at home with the
children. These thirteen women had spent an average of six
years at home with their children and were thus probably not
like the typical reentry woman, who has spent the major portion of her adult years raising a family before returning to work
outside the home. Quite possibly, the problems surrounding reentry would be even more severe for women who have been unemployed for longer periods.

Only two of these thirteen families experienced little or
no difficulty with the woman's return to work. In eleven families, six men apparently favored their wives' return to work but
then later became critical of their work, while five had mixed
feelings and resisted their wives' employment.

Attitudes about the desirability of women's work fluctuated over time. Men who began the marriage not wanting their wives to work changed their minds as the children grew older and financial burdens increased. Some women who had been in the home for several years were a bit reluctant to enter the work world again. They had not kept up with their careers or had no career to which they could return. Or they had simply lost confidence in their ability to work outside the home. Sometimes the courage to reenter the work world came only after they had pursued some volunteer activity or interest outside the home:

Sue: After a while, he wanted me to go to work so we could have more money. And I didn't want to. I didn't want to go to work. First of all, I didn't know what to do, anything I thought I could do, I wouldn't get paid very well . . . I didn't want to teach again . . . Then I got very interested in modern dancing and I went every day, and he was very resentful that I would do that. It started taking me away from him and the family . . . I was just finding out that I had things exciting to me and I loved it. I made my body nicer, and I was stronger, and it gave me a lot of joy. And he did not like that at all . . . After I decided I couldn't be a dancer forever and ever, I started part-time work as a secretary. Then I decided I needed more money, and that was when I started working . . . First I had to do this dance thing. I found out as an individual I had something I could do for myself.

As a woman reentered the work world and became excited about her own development, her husband's attitudes changed. Conflict arose as he began complaining about the number of hours she spent away from home or her failure to take care of housekeeping chores.

Often the conflict was expressed covertly rather than openly. Perhaps resistance was covert because the real issue was not the woman's employment *per se* but the subtle and complex changes that occurred in her as a result of this employment. Women found that work enlarged their world. They gained new female friends and met men who were attractive to them. They also became more confident in themselves and began to demand more from their husbands. Men felt vaguely threatened by these changes but seemed either unable or unwilling to acknowledge this threat. Some men expressed their resentment by withdrawing from the relationship. Jeff discussed his difficulties in accepting his wife's return to graduate school and acknowledged that this event had coincided with his extramarital affair:

Jeff: I resented a lot of things. She went back to graduate school; I resented her doing that even though I had intellectualized and wanted her to get out and go to work. I was used to having a dependent person with me.

Interviewer: When she went back to graduate school, what were you concerned about?

Jeff: I really don't know. I just remember that at that point I felt it coincided with a lot of things. I felt affection was being taken away from me. I had an affair at that time—there were a whole lot of things that were antirelationship.

Tensions about work also surfaced in disputes about the housework. Although men agreed that with their wives' full-time work outside the home, more of the household chores should be shared, they resisted taking full responsibility for half the work. Frequently they would insist on doing only those tasks that appealed to them or were least distasteful. Some men chose to do the shopping; others offered to help with the food preparation. Some specifically mentioned laundry or housecleaning chores that they absolutely refused to share. Not only a dislike for the task but a need to resist the wife's demand stimulated this vehement refusal to share chores. Men understood the source of their wives' new strength and assertiveness but resisted yielding to demands and losing control within the relationship. As Kevin described it:

Kevin: Virginia was all of a sudden demanding that I do half the housework . . . It wasn't so much the housework; I didn't really mind that. It was more that she felt her own importance all of a sudden.

Interviewer: What kinds of things did she ask you to do around the house?

Kevin: Just all the usual stuff, clothes, cleaning, dishes. I had always helped with the dishes and done a lot of cleaning anyway. The clothes I had never been too crazy about. Basically I refused to do that.

To some men, capitulating to a demand signified weakness. As Don stated:

Don: Oh, dishes are okay, that's cool. But when she starts asking me to do the vacuuming and things, I said, "That's your job!" . . . I started feeling messed up. I didn't want to be a marshmallow. I'm not going to do all of it. "You do it." . . . You know, I got to a point where I'd be very strong and say, "No, you gotta do this stuff. You gotta do it."

Another problem that bothered both the women who worked consistently throughout the marriage and those who reentered the work force was the second-class nature of their work. Women complained that their husbands wanted them to work for the benefits this work brought to the family, but they did not take the woman's work seriously and did not expect her to develop a career. Or, if she developed a career, it was subordinate to the man's career. When asked how her husband responded to her work, Nancy remarked:

Nancy: Greg only wanted me to work when it was appropriate or convenient. When we wanted to buy a house, he wanted me to go back to work. When we needed the money and he was in medical school, it was all right for me to work. He saw my work just as a means to an end, as far as things for the family. He felt I should be at home with the girls and with him and for him. My role was that of hostess, wife, mistress, lover

—this was my role. It was not to be out as a career woman.

Sheryl, who taught at the same university as her husband, concluded:

Sheryl: On the surface he was always encouraging. He said from the start that he was happy to have his wife working . . . He would say, "Yes, this is very good, I like what you're doing." But there was always the feeling that what he was doing was more valuable. If it came to a choice which of us was going to get a job, it was understood, and for a couple of years it was the case, that he was the one whose interests had to be satisfied. So the idea was that it was all right for me to work as long as I was not in direct competition with him. As soon as there was any possibility that my doing something might detract from him, I think that he got very nervous. The underlying cause of the final separation was the threat that I was actually taking over, not taking over, but surpassing him.

Obviously, employment meant more than a job. It was not the job itself that created problems for these marriages; men seemed quite willing, in fact, to agree on the desirability of employment for women. But even those who wholeheartedly supported the principle of employment had difficulty with the reality of that work for their own wives. A new assertiveness and strength within the woman challenged male dominance and created conflict over the issue of control.

The Dedicated Worker. Both men and women acknowledged that the husband's work had also created difficulties within the marriage. Basically, the complaints centered on two very different kinds of problems. Some women complained that the man's work involved a commitment in time and/or emotional participation that detracted from his participation in family life. In other families, couples experienced conflict when the husband was judged as underachieving; he wasn't earning enough money, or he became unemployed and lost jobs during the marriage.

The most frequently mentioned problem, however, involved the first type—the dedicated worker, who was too involved with his work. Women's complaints about their husband's involvement in his work sometimes focused simply on the time he put into his work. The hours he spent on the job prevented him from participating in or giving much to the family; or he wouldn't take enough time off for vacations. However, often the commitment was not measured simply by time. Wives resented their husbands' emotional involvement in their jobs. Beth said her husband did not work too many hours but took his work home with him emotionally:

Interviewer: What about his work? Was it ever a source of friction?

Beth: Yes.

Interviewer: In what way?

Beth: He was always under pressure and he brought that pressure home. He would never relax and forget about that awhile. I would say, "Let's do something. You can't do anything about it tonight, and let's not think about it." He often brought the problems home from work, and he alienated me more with his wanting time to think about it. He wanted to be alone most of the time. I always had to just coax him into giving me some time and attention . . .

Interviewer: Did he ever talk about what was bothering him?

Beth: No. He said I wouldn't understand, there's just too much to talk about, and he didn't want to go over this.

Ralph, a trial lawyer, discussed the impact his work had on the marriage:

Interviewer: What was the chief problem in your marriage?

Ralph: Probably I just got involved in work. There were

	a lot of pressures in terms of the nature of the work . . . I feel strongly about it. There's a certain ideology that goes with it, a certain bitterness. You get upset. You don't get upset with the problem or the boss. You get upset with the nature of the thing itself.
Interviewer:	Because the issues are so important and affect people's lives?
Ralph:	Yeah, everything has tremendous effect. You are not talking about fining someone $500 or getting something in on time. You are basically saying whether someone is going to prison or not. Sometimes they are in prison for a long time. Plus, there is a lot of friction in the trial. You don't know the outcomes . . . It is physically tiring. I would not be surprised if it is the most exhausting occupation . . .
Interviewer:	So I suppose you would come home feeling the effects of your work. Did you find then that it was difficult for her to understand that?
Ralph:	She understood that, but she didn't like it. It's kind of hard when you are in trial and you come home. You are on what I call "The Nod." When someone is talking to you, you don't hear and you go like this [nodding head]. With your tension level you become less tolerant of anybody that you feel does not support you. . . . She found me unresponsive to her and the children.

Since several of the men in the interview sample had very demanding jobs, commitment to work was frequently recognized as a problem by both men and women. In approximately one fourth of the families, the respondents talked about the demands of the husbands' jobs and their impact on the family, especially the wife. She often ended up feeling left out, deprived, or less important to her husband than his job.

The Underachiever. A second type of complaint was quite different from the first. In about 20 percent of the homes, the complaints focused on the inadequacy of the husband's employment. The wife disliked the job he had or felt he could get a better one or was not making enough money. Women indicated they did not confront their husbands with their feelings about their work, but two men in this group said they were aware of their wives' dissatisfaction with some element of their careers. Five of the men in this group either quit working or lost their jobs during the marriage. For four of these men, the periods of unemployment were brief, and they continued seeking work. One man, however, did not work during the entire period of the marriage. The roles in this family were reversed, the woman supporting the family and the man taking care of the child.

For most of these forty families, employment of either the husband or the wife was not in itself the problem. Time spent on the job, salary, or responsibilities were seldom the most troublesome issues. Work served as an indirect source of conflict, as it affected perceptions of self and the partner and the status of each partner within the relationship. Shifts in employment were often accompanied by shifts of power within the marriage. Work also affected the security of the marriage when it was perceived as commanding a greater emotional commitment than the marriage itself. Because it touched on the couple's security and status with each other, employment became a key issue for many of these families.

The Sexual Relationship

The sexual relationship within the marriage was a second source of difficulty. Only 25 percent of the men and women interviewed viewed their sexual relationship as satisfactory or good; the others felt it presented major or minor problems within the marriage. Men complained that their wives were not responsive enough. They described their marriages as inhibited; their wives, and occasionally they themselves, had not had enough experience before the marriage. Other men felt not enough time and attention had been given to sex during the marriage.

When they talked about what would improve sex for

them, about one third of the men indicated that problems
stemmed from their wives' lack of responsiveness; they attrib-
uted this unresponsiveness to deep-seated psychological problems that could be treated only through therapy.

A few men, who felt their sexual problems were related
to other problems within the marriage, believed sex would have
improved only if these problems had been corrected. The re-
mainder of the men suggested a wide variety of tactics for improving sex, from better birth control to more communication
to more experience. Men, therefore, were about equally divided
between those who felt the sexual problems were related to
some difficulties within the marriage and those who perceived
their wives' psychological difficulties as the source of the sexual
problem.

In discussing their sexual relationship, some women acknowledged they had not been responsive to their husbands and
characterized their relationship as inhibited. Other women complained about the lack of affection within the marriage.

Women differed from men, however, when they talked
about methods for improving sex. They emphasized the connection between the sexual problems and other problems within
the marriage. For example, four women specifically mentioned
the husband's control of the sexual relationship as troublesome.
They felt he controlled sex just as he controlled the rest of the
marriage. They resented this control and were sexually unrespon-
sive. Nancy explained:

Interviewer: What did you feel was the problem in the times
                 you didn't feel responsive?
Nancy: . . . Whenever he wanted to have sex, I had to be
                 there. I wasn't allowed to say, "I'm not inter-
                 ested or tired or don't want to right now."

Beth felt it was very difficult to get her husband to give
her what she needed for satisfaction:

Beth: I thought before I married him that he was just nervous
          or something. He just couldn't relax. At times he was
          okay, but I always had to do things the way he wanted

and not the way I wanted. I'd say, "Glen, can you go a little slower?" He was always very fast, very rough and quick, no foreplay at all really ... He would always blame me. I said, "It is hard to turn on when you go so fast." It was hard for me to talk to him because I never wanted to make him feel that it was his fault ... I would say "If you could just go a little slower, I could get into the mood, for doing anything," and I could have. I wasn't even turned on half the time and it was over. I lay there and he went to sleep ... There were times when he really tried to be loving and kind and affectionate, but there was something that always held him back. He could never let go. "Let's just enjoy each other." If I said something like that, he would tighten up altogether, so I could never really talk to him about it. He wouldn't let me. He would cut me off.

Some women felt their sexual problems would be solved only when other problems within the marriage were resolved. Doris described different approaches typically taken by the male and female in resolving sexual and marital problems:

Doris: We weren't able to just put our problems on the shelf. He thought if we could sleep together, these other things would go away, and I maintained these other things would have to be okay before I could.

In summary, although both men and women acknowledged that their sexual relationships had not been very satisfactory, their views of the problem and its solution were different. Men more frequently tended to see sexual problems as caused by psychological problems or inhibitory factors dating from earlier years. Women more frequently linked the sexual problems with current difficulties in the relationship; their sex life suffered when problems within the marriage remained unresolved.

Impact of Children on the Marriage

Children had a profound effect on these marriages. While parents recognized children had enriched their lives and their marriages, they also felt children had created difficulties in the relationship. The three most critical elements were failures in family planning, the disruptive impact of the first child, and difficulties in child rearing.

Family Planning. Family planning posed problems for twenty of the forty families. Thirty-four of the seventy-eight children (44 percent) born to these forty families were not planned. A small group of families, however, had most difficulty in planning. Eight families had between two and five unplanned children each and accounted for twenty-two of the thirty-four unplanned children.

Men and women acknowledged that failure in planning occurred either because they did not use birth control or because they used it erratically. Some families did not use birth control even when they knew children could create a major disruption in their plans. Very young unmarried couples who were not established in their careers and were still in school made little attempt to prevent birth of children. Women who had three or four children had one more, even though they acknowledged that they were already overloaded and could hardly handle what they had. One couple had been warned by their physician that potential hemorrhaging might cause death for the woman if she had a fourth child. But they continued without contraceptives, and she had a fourth child. In each of these situations, threats of potential disruption, physical harm, and possibly even death did not cause the couple to take the necessary precautions.

In several families, a kind of fatalistic attitude prevailed in matters of childbirth and family planning. Neither the husband nor the wife attempted to control their situation. They did not even discuss the issue with each other.

Ultimately, however, success or failure in planning had little relation to the couple's acceptance of the child. Some families who established a pattern of having children with no effort to plan accepted these children without any apparent difficulties. Children were received positively; the couple made efforts to control conception only after they felt their family was established, with three or four children. These people accepted children as a necessary, inevitable part of marriage and family life and felt no need to control the timing or spacing of their arrival.

However, careful planning for a child and delight with the conception did not always guarantee a positive response to either the pregnancy period or the infant's arrival. Some women who had been most eager to have a child found that their feelings changed and became more negative during the pregnancy or immediately after the birth.

The First Child. The conception and pregnancy of the first child had a powerful impact on men and women. In particular, two conditions—marital status and planning—affected men's and women's responses. In eight families the conception occurred before the couple were married, in seven families the couple were married but the child was not planned, and in twenty-three families the couple were married and the child was planned. Two couples adopted their first child; they will not be included in this discussion on planning.

The men and women in the forced-marriage situation understandably reported the most distressed feelings about the pregnancy. It created hardships for them because in several cases they were not planning to marry; they were in school and were not established in careers. The commitment to the relationship was weak, and the timing created serious problems.

For the couples who were already married but not planning a child, the responses were more mixed, with some positive responses occurring. The timing in these marriages presented some problems to four of the seven couples. The husband was not established in his career, and in one family he was still in school. These four families also indicated they would have liked to have more time to just enjoy their life together. In the other three families the husband had already completed his education and begun his career. Financial problems in these three families were minimal.

In the twenty-three families in which the child was planned, finances were more secure and the couple felt emotionally ready to assume responsibility for a child. However, in four of these families, one partner talked the other into having a child, and there was more ambivalence about the conception.

In summary, men and women responded similarly to conception of the first child. Their emotional responses, which ranged from despair to joy, were related primarily to whether they were married and whether the conception was planned or accidental.

Although men's and women's reactions to the news of the conception of the first child tended to be similar, their responses to the pregnancy were different. For about half the men, the period prior to the child's birth had no substantial effect on them and did not result in any changes in their lives. But most of the women (84 percent) experienced substantial changes in their lives; the pregnancy affected their work, activities, and emotions.

In particular, the pregnancy had a strong impact on women emotionally. When respondents were asked, "What effect did the pregnancy have upon you and your spouse?," they more frequently recalled women's problems. Responses indicated that fourteen of the thirty-eight women (37 percent) experienced emotional distress, including depression, anger, anxiety, loneliness, but only eight of the men (21 percent) had similar feelings during this period. These numbers are based on spontaneous recall and most likely underestimate the amount of emotional distress during pregnancy. Quite likely a higher proportion of persons with some emotional difficulties would have been recorded if the question had specifically inquired about emotional states during the pregnancy period.

Most of the men experiencing distress during this period were still adjusting to an unplanned event. They were not secure in the couple relationship, and they were anxious about the extra financial burden the child would place on them. For women, however, whether the child was planned did not affect their emotional responses. About one third of the women who had planned the pregnancy experienced some depression and anxiety during this period. These negative feelings surprised and concerned them.

The differences in male and female perceptions that began to develop during the pregnancy were accentuated after the birth of the first child. Men seldom reported stress following the birth of the child. Even those men who had not planned a child and who had married because of the pregnancy seldom experienced difficulties related to the arrival and care of the infant.

Apparently, men with unplanned families initially experienced some distress at the news of the conception; in some cases they were forced into a marriage or a change of plans for work and school. Some experienced emotional difficulties during the period before the child's birth. However, few of these men found the time following the birth of the child stressful.

Within this group there were, however, a few exceptions. Some men who had not planned to have a child were still in school or preparing for a career after the child arrived. They felt frustrated with the conflicting demands on their time, energy, and commitment:

Interviewer: So you were not planning to have a child then?

Kevin: It was an accidental pregnancy . . . If I had children, I wanted to be in a financial position to handle it. Somehow I knew there was more to it when you had a child—more money, more demand. I knew that if I went to school and had a child and a wife, my time was going to be cut in half. And I think once Brad came, even though I cared for him a lot, it was really a frustrating situation. Because I had to divide my time, and I found myself staying up until two and three o'clock in the morning studying, and getting up in the morning and going to work. I think it was a real prime time for me, and I wasn't probably the most understanding person. I was probably irritable a lot. I was in a hurry because I felt I wanted to finish school and I wasn't able to. I dropped out a semester here just because it would get too heavy. I would feel I should spend more time with the family. I dropped out, and then I would get frustrated because I wasn't going anywhere. I can see why it happened. I know why the situation turned up the way it did.

I had a goal and it was being frustrated. No matter which way I went, it was frustrated.

For women in the unplanned-family situations, the arrival of the child heightened the pressure they had been experiencing. Women who were not ready for pregnancy and perhaps not ready for a marriage, who experienced emotional distress during the pregnancy, were most severely affected by the new responsibilities imposed on them by the infant.

Among the families in which the pregnancy was planned, men reported very little stress following the birth of the child. They tended to report the birth as a very natural process, with maybe a little lost sleep and some inefficiency in meals or housekeeping, but basically they experienced no big changes with the arrival of the infant. They generally felt happy about the child and had relatively little stress with the entire process. After the baby arrived, only minor adjustments were necessary. The process of conception, pregnancy, and birth gave them feelings of pride, pleasure, and achievement.

Women who planned their children and were delighted with the conception did not proceed evenly through the process. Some began to experience some emotional difficulties during the pregnancy. They began to feel anxious and tense. After the child's birth, some women had very mixed reactions. They were proud and happy to have the child but were also confronted with unexpected but very intense negative emotions. They had looked forward to the child's birth and were now surprised to find themselves depressed, anxious, and desperate. They were not prepared for these feelings.

Thus, men and women reported very different kinds of experiences with conception, pregnancy, and birth of the first child. The diversity of these experiences was revealed in the language and style of responses used by men and women during the interviews. Many men had some difficulties remembering their feelings and the events surrounding the birth of the first child. They used matter-of-fact statements indicating it was a normal process in which everything went as expected. Emotions, if any, were muted; they were pleasurable feelings of pride and happiness.

The following are typical responses men made when asked about their experiences in the month after the baby's birth:

Sidney: I remember I was pretty happy after the baby was born. Everything was okay. There wasn't anything traumatic. Nothing stands out in my mind.

Interviewer: What effect did the baby have upon your relationship?
Ken: Nothing. There were the normal changes after the baby was born.
Interviewer: What kinds of changes?
Ken: Rescheduling around child and reordering priorities.

Larry: I was in training [Air Force] at the time. Oh, the standard stuff you go through, the adjustments you make for having a new person in the house and especially a very demanding person. It's been so many years ago.
Interviewer: Yes, it has.
Larry: There was nothing in particular. It's just a normal thing, you have a baby in the house. It's going to change everything to a degree.

Women, however, did not recall the birth as some far distant, dimly remembered event but as one that might have happened yesterday. It appeared very fresh in their memories; they recalled very specific events. Adjectives with intense emotional coloring were used to describe the events and feelings. Themes occurring most frequently in the women's conversations were the isolation, loneliness, and overwhelming sense of responsibility associated with having a child. Sue talked about her baby's arrival shortly after they had moved to a new neighborhood where she did not know anyone:

Interviewer: What do you recall of your experiences during the first month after the baby was born?

Sue: I was depressed, tired, happy, and pleased to have this beautiful little boy.

Interviewer: Do you know what set off the depression?

Sue: I think it was physically caused. I felt tired. I was tired and up a lot. The baby didn't sleep. I felt kind of desperate. There was a lot of anxiety . . . I didn't have any friends, and I hated it there. We lived quite a ways from town, and I had one friend who lived twenty-five minutes away. It was hard to get together. I never had a baby-sitter.

Interviewer: You were isolated, then.

Sue: I was very isolated. We were way out. I had a car, but what is the use of picking up my baby and going? I had no place to go.

Interviewer: You didn't get babysitters? Was that because you were concerned about the care?

Sue: I didn't know how to get them. I didn't know anybody around to ask. There wasn't anybody around. It was empty around there.

Ann Marie talked about the isolation she felt. She had worked in a clerical position, and she did not miss her job, but she did miss the stimulation and contact with people that the job gave her:

Interviewer: What do you recall of your experiences the first month after the baby was born?

Ann Marie: Exhausting, wondered what I had done. I felt totally tied down, strapped to this person. Lots of responsibility . . .

Interviewer: Did you miss your work?

Ann Marie: I didn't know if I missed my work as much as the people contact.

The adjustment to the first child was difficult even for women who did not give up their jobs. Sheryl talked about her efforts to combine child rearing with her college teaching:

Sheryl: I remember the first ten days when I was staying home with him just about drove me mad. I was really not happy at being confined to the house and not being able to get out when I wanted to. All the fears that I had always had about the confining nature of motherhood seemed to be realized. Fortunately we were within easy walking distance of our offices, and what I eventually learned to do after the first couple confining weeks was put the baby in a carriage and wheel him into the office. Then I had some great idea that he would be a reasonable baby and sleep while I wrote all those papers I had to write. I did work out a scheme whereby I learned to nurse him with one hand and type my papers with the other. But it didn't quite work out that way. They are heavier than you think [laughs].

Whatever the woman's situation, whether she was in a foreign country, a suburban neighborhood, or a university setting, she often reported feelings of anxiety and fear. Many women felt overwhelmed by a sense of being totally responsible for the child. It was a responsibility they could not really share or turn over to anyone else. The husband was gone most of the time; but even when he was home and helpful in caring for the child, the woman was anxious. Babysitters were either unavailable or not trusted. Ultimately, many women felt a desperate sense of helplessness because they were totally responsible for the infant but had little sense of control.

Child Rearing. The third source of difficulty with children was in child rearing. Different approaches to managing and caring for the children created conflict in all but five homes. In about half the homes (twenty-one, or 52.5 percent) the conflict was mild, and the couple experienced only occasional difficulties. However, in about 35 percent of the families (fourteen), different attitudes toward disciplining and nurturing the children provoked serious conflict and continued as a major unresolved problem within the marriage.

Conflict most often centered on different styles of management. One parent frequently felt the other was too strict or too permissive or not consistent enough. In a few families the primary issue was nurturance; one parent complained that the other spouse was not emotionally responsive to the children.

Men and women reported some differences in child-rearing behaviors. More fathers were perceived as having some form of firm control, ranging from an issue-oriented, reasoning approach to an authoritarian approach based on authority and obedience. Only a few men were characterized as permissive. About three fourths of the women were perceived as having some form of firm control, and about one fourth were seen as permissive.

In the interviews, men and women talked differently about child rearing. Women more frequently acknowledged that they or their husbands yelled or lost their tempers with their children. They described incidents in which children were beaten or punished severely by either parent. These incidents provoked shame, anxiety, and remorse.

Men seldom reported these kinds of incidents. They tended to talk about child rearing in a problem-solving, issue-oriented manner; they presented it as a rational process. They seldom referred to any kinds of emotional acts, such as either parent yelling, screaming, spanking, or beating. Furthermore, they tended to give less time in the interview to discussing the children's problems. They gave less information on child rearing and fewer examples of family incidents.

Marriage presented very different realities for these men and women. Although they shared similar dreams and hopes for intimacy and companionship and were similarly disappointed over their failures to achieve these dreams, they recalled very different kinds of experiences. They agreed that work, sex, and children presented major problems, but they differed markedly in their descriptions and interpretations of these problems. Perhaps this inability to construct a common or shared definition and interpretation of family life contributed to the eventual failure of these marriages.

3

Hostility and Avoidance in Long-Term Marriages

During the course of marriage, men and women established styles of interaction. They created patterns of behaviors that were cumulative. Their behaviors at the time of divorce were based on this sequence of acts and responses.

Each family had its own unique history, but a comparison of families revealed similarities among these forty families. Using a fairly elaborate scheme of behaviors, I was able to place thirty-nine families into six groups (see Appendix: Research Notes for a more detailed description of procedures used in grouping families). One family was clearly unique and did not fit easily into any of the six groups. This particular family had a Latin background. The husband and wife had reversed roles during their marriage; he had remained home with the child, and the wife had worked throughout the marriage. The reversal of roles contributed to the development of a very different marital pattern. Since their style of interaction was too dissimilar to others, this family was dropped from further analysis.

After grouping families on the basis of interactive behaviors, I examined groups to see whether these families exhibited other similarities and differences. Were the families in one pattern, for example, older or younger than the families in other groups? Did they differ in family size and composition?

Table 5 indicates that families in the six groups differed significantly in several ways. Fragile Bond and Fractured Families tended to be older couples with school-age and teenage children. They had an average of two or three children, but a couple of these families were quite large, with four or even five children. These families were complete, as neither husbands nor wives were considering having more children. Doll's House and Stalemate Marriages tended to be a little younger. Most of these parents were in their thirties, and their children were school age. The Perfect Model and Unformed Families were the youngest families. Perfect Model families generally had preschool and occasionally young school-age children. Unformed Families were the most youthful, with men and women in their twenties, and married an average of only three years. For some of these families, divorce may have interrupted family formation; some of these men and women indicated a desire for more children.

These significant differences suggest that marital behaviors are linked with other family characteristics. Older men and women reported different styles of behavior, which, in turn, reflected differences in attitudes about marriage and family life. A commitment to traditional roles in marriage, for example, affected not only the division of work and responsibility but also the couple's interactive style. Younger families differed not only in family size and age of children; they adopted different styles of relating to each other, which, to some degree, reflected different attitudes about family life.

Fragile Bond Marriages

Larry: We just went in different directions. Somehow there was a point at which she wanted to emulate her mother . . . and just be the housewife mother for the kids. I

Table 5. Stages of Life Cycle and Family Size in Six Family Groups.

Life Cycle and Family Size	Family Group					
	Fragile Bond (N = 6)	Fractured Families (N = 10)	Doll's House (N = 8)	Stalemate (N = 4)	Perfect Model (N = 8)	Unformed Families (N = 3)
Husband's Average Age	45.1	40.4	38.0	35.8	32.7	26.3
Wife's Average Age[a]	40.3	37.7	36.7	33.5	30.5	24.3
Average Age of Oldest Child[b]	12.6	10.8	10.3	9.7	4.5	2.0
Length of Marriage[c]	16.6	13.4	12.8	10.3	7.4	3.0
Number of Children	2.2	2.4	2.1	1.8	1.5	1.3

[a]Analysis of Variance, $F = 4.06$, 38 d.f., $p < .006$
[b]Analysis of Variance, $F = 7.89$, 38 d.f., $p < .0001$
[c]Analysis of Variance, $F = 3.51$, 38 d.f., $p < .01$

still wanted the lady companion that I had had. And
she didn't have any time for me. When I would come
home, and wanted to talk to her, she was not available
to talk to me because she was so busy with the dinner.
And yet if one of the women from the neighborhood
came over, she could abandon the kitchen and go in
and sip a glass of sherry with the lady. I got resentful
in that I felt I was being deserted for a role that was
beneath her and certainly beneath what we had set for
ourselves earlier.

Janice: I don't think our interactions were all that great . . .
He is hard to talk to. He always has been. He wouldn't
talk. He would get bored or tired.

Larry and Janice expressed views commonly found in
these six Fragile Bond marriages. Marriages that began with a
full promise of love and commitment did not develop the way
each person had hoped. Because of their separate work roles
and their difficulty in expressing their emotions, these men and
women created separate worlds for themselves.

They never struggled with each other to create a common
world. In silence, they allowed their frustrations to accumulate.
As they avoided confrontation on disturbing issues, they drifted
apart emotionally. Even though they lived together for many
years, and their marriages appeared stable, the bonds uniting
them were fragile, brittle, and vulnerable. Eventually these
bonds were broken when one partner chose to walk away from
the marriage.

In addition to their avoidance patterns, Fragile Bond families differed from other families in their approach to marital
roles, their age, and length of time they had been married.
These six families were older and more traditional than the
other families. Men in this group averaged forty-five and women
forty at the time of divorce. They had been married an average
of seventeen years. All their children were at least school age,
and most were teenagers.

In keeping with their traditional values, men developed a

career and women assumed primary responsibility for the home and family. If the wife did work, she worked only when the family needed extra funds. The women's primary commitment was to mothering; all six women were very child-oriented.

Separating and Substituting. Men and women in the Fragile Bond families gave very little thought to how they should behave as husbands and wives. They seemed to move effortlessly into patterns they had learned in their childhood from their own parents. Kathy learned about priorities in life from her family and church:

Interviewer: Do you think the children's arrival had any effect upon your work life or goals?

Kathy: No, they didn't, because of my upbringing in the church. I felt the primary responsibility and priority was my family. Working was secondary to me.

Bob was proud of his ability to support his family. He had learned how important this was from his father:

Bob: Like my father, I didn't want Mary Ann to work. I felt it was degrading.

Interviewer: Why was that?

Bob: It reflected on my ability to provide. It was a very strong thing with my parents. My mother did not work, and my father would just not hear of it. And my wife was brought up that way too— her mother didn't work either. Now that I look back on it, and now that I read about it, I think it may have been the best thing for our marriage if she had worked.

As these marriages progressed, both men and women began to resent these traditional divisions of work. Women felt their husbands separated themselves from the family and spent too much time and energy working. Men complained about their wives' devoting too much of their attention to the children and not enough to them. With some humor, Janice described her husband's devotion to his teaching and research:

Interviewer: Was his work ever a source of friction?
Janice: . . . I thought he spent too much time at it. That's all he did. In a way his desk to me was like a giant pacifier, like a play station that he could not be separated from. I saw him mostly from his back, sitting at a desk.

Kathy resented not only her husband's long hours spent in work but his refusal to communicate about his experiences:

Kathy: I always asked him when he came in, "How was your day? What happened today?" Or "How was your presentation?" Oh, he would say, "It was all right," or "It was a heavy day." I would say, "Well, what was your presentation about?" And he would say, "I don't know," or "It's too much to talk about." Every time I asked him about the business, trying to become involved through him because I didn't know any other way to find out what he actually did, he wouldn't talk about it.

Men in the Fragile Bond marriages defended their lack of communication by explaining how hard it was to communicate with wives who didn't work. As Bob perceived it, he and Mary Ann lived in separate worlds:

Bob: It was a typical situation in which she was a housewife, and I had a job. I could come home and tell her about it, but I'm sure it wouldn't have the impact on her as it would if I were talking to someone who had worked that day . . . If she had put in a day's work and we had gone together, she would have understood more. And vice versa, of course. I wasn't up on what her problems would have been through the day with the child.

Traditional roles that divided men's and women's work and separated them in their daily living had some unpleasant consequences for men as well as for women. Some men felt locked into their careers; they felt they could not risk changes that entailed possible temporary declines in income or unemployment. Bob spoke with some regrets of lost opportunities to launch into a business partnership:

Bob: I didn't have the flexibility some people had. Where if I didn't like what I was doing, I could just say, "To hell with it," and look for something that I really thought would work out. Nor did I ever have an opportunity in my life to say, "Maybe I could go into business for myself." You almost have to start from ground zero at that point. I had a family, a son and a daughter, and I can't do that . . . I thought about starting a partnership, but it would have been a little slow at first, and we would have had a harder time making ends meet. My wife working would have given me that opportunity, but I didn't want her to work.

Several men also complained about their wives' overinvolvement with the home and children. Just as women complained about the husband's commitment to work, the men felt women sought too much attention and affection from their children. The time and attention women gave to their children deprived the men of the affection and interest they felt was their right within the marriage. They understood, of course, that their children deserved attention, but they resented it. Ralph felt there was little opportunity for privacy with children in the house:

Ralph: Jacky gave a lot of herself to the children. That becomes as important; the energy is not devoted entirely to me, obviously. It is shared.

Interviewer: I suppose there must have been times when you felt that there wasn't enough time and energy to go around.

Ralph: Oh, sure. You're always concerned with the kids. When you want to spend Sunday afternoon with your wife alone, they come in, "Daddy or Mommy, can I do this?" And she is so child-oriented that it is basically an open house.

Interviewer: No privacy?

Ralph: No privacy. Kids are always welcome. And even if there's privacy, it's not real privacy. It's the illusion of privacy, because the kids are always out there. The truth of the matter is that as long as they are in the house and you are in the house, there is really no privacy.

In addition to not sharing their work loads, men and women in Fragile Bond marriages became separated from each other emotionally. They were not spontaneous in expressing their feelings of affection, tenderness, anger, or grief. Sometimes anger was never expressed. Janice talked about her attempts to locate her anger at the end of the marriage:

Interviewer: At the time of your separation, were you angry or depressed?

Janice: Anger, I couldn't find any anger. A lot of depression. I thought, "Where is my anger? I can't even locate it."

Interviewer: Were you ever able to? Did you ever get angry?

Janice: Oh, sure. I don't know about straightforward anger, a lot of smoldering.

Sorrow and grief were also not expressed. Mary Ann and Bob had the tragic experience of three children who did not survive birth. Two were stillborn, but the third lived for a brief time after birth. Bob recalled:

Bob: I comforted Mary Ann but comforted her in a way that was apparently the wrong way for her. We tried to ignore the situation. It wasn't until a year or so ago, when the marriage was on the rocks, that I learned that she thought I was heartless about the situation. Here I was crying at night but not wanting her to know that I felt that because I didn't want to upset her. She seemed to be holding something in; neither one of us knew how the other felt.

Thus, both husbands and wives in Fragile Bond marriages did not connect emotionally and withheld their feelings from each other. Of course, when they began their married life, they never intended to live in a way that created distance between them. They were simply following cultural patterns they had learned from their own parents. Only after some time in the marriage did these gestures of separation result in feelings of deprivation. As they felt deprived of closeness, they intensified their search for substitute satisfactions in children and work.

Couples were reluctant to discuss these feelings with each other. Perhaps they felt they had no *right* to feel deprived. The wife may have reasoned that she should not fault her husband for his commitment to work; she knew long hours were essential for advancement in his career. She really could not criticize him for taking his role of providing for the family *too* seriously. Her husband was annoyed with her commitment to homemaking and mothering, but how could he complain about this? How could he fault her for being *too* attentive a parent? Couples were thus trapped; they were very responsible in fulfilling their family roles. It was not their failure to be responsible that triggered distress; rather, marital distress was caused by the unintended emotional deprivation resulting from this unexamined commitment to traditional roles.

In addition, they had little skill in assessing and expressing their own feelings. It was much easier to forget nagging irritations and bury their frustrations. Their failure to confront each other intensified the emotional distance between them.

Subtracting and Leaving. Lack of emotional spontaneity gave Fragile Bond Marriages a low, flat profile. There were few moments of either intense, passionate joy or despair. Men and women experienced their marriages as rather quiet and subdued. They maintained a deceptive tranquility by steadfastly refusing to address uncomfortable issues. Over time, the couple shared fewer areas of life. Janice described this process of *subtracting*:

Janice: The first time I realized that anything was wrong was when Cliff arranged for himself to go alone on that first sabbatical to Asia.

Interviewer: When you found out he was making that trip, what was your response? What did you do or say?

Janice: I withdrew. I was so shocked; it was like our first divorce. I realized he would do things without thinking of me...After that, something snapped. And how often does that happen to people?

Interviewer: What do you mean?

Janice: I mean this kind of cordoning off an area that you just don't talk about anymore. Where you just subtract and subtract and what do you have left? Just this little area.

Interviewer: It's like peeling an onion!

Janice: Yeah, the people I talk to, I thought this was kind of unique, but it happens a lot. And the reasons can be infinite. It can be someone didn't get you a glass of water, when you asked them.

Because small cracks were concealed, these marriages appeared very stable to the couple, to their children, and to the community. The stability, however, was deceptive; these marriages all ended very abruptly with little flamboyance or passionate anger. While on a sabbatical, Cliff wrote a letter to Janice, indicating his intention to initiate a divorce on his return. Larry simply left a note on the living room table and walked out one day, with no prior explanation or argument. The partners who did not initiate the separation appeared in every case to be completely unprepared for it. They had not defined their marriages as troubled; none of the couples had sought counseling.

In the period immediately after the divorce, husbands and wives were troubled by disturbing thoughts. They wondered whether they had ever really known each other. They realized they successfully avoided the threat of conflict within their marriage, but they also failed to establish any deep connections or bonds. *Their marital bonds were fragile.* Over time, the marriage became a superficial shell, functional, useful, apparently whole, but brittle and vulnerable. Eventually, with only a minor incident acting as a trigger, the marriage shattered abruptly and unexpectedly.

The Family Divides. Because these long-term, outwardly stable marriages ended so abruptly, men and women suffered a great deal of pain through the separation and postdivorce period. They frequently reported long periods of depression and difficulty in functioning. Bob became very despondent and considered suicide. Janice withdrew and remained in her house, sleeping for long periods.

Adjustment was further hindered because many men and women in these Fragile Bond marriages had quite limited support systems outside their marriage. They had as much difficulty cultivating intimacy with persons outside their marriage as they had with their mates. Most had only one relative or a few friends they could talk to about their divorce. After the divorce Roger and Bob found church groups with whom they could relate. Kathy found a church leader helpful but felt uncomfortable with fellow members, most of whom had never experienced divorce. Eventually she stopped going to church. None of the men or women belonged to a same-sex support group. When questioned about this, Janice acknowledged that such a group might be useful but not at this point:

Interviewer:	Did you participate in any women's support groups?
Janice:	No.
Interviewer:	Was it just because you didn't feel it was anything you needed or wanted?
Janice:	No, I would like it, but I just felt that the priorities were survival. That would be a luxury. I don't mean just economic survival, but psychic survival. Of course, that's what you go to these groups for. But there is something before that,

something between you and yourself. I would still like to do those things. But the time is not right yet.

Some, like Kathy, found that this need to cope with internal stress and a definite preference for privacy led to a period of withdrawal after the divorce.

Interviewer: Did you belong to any other groups?
Kathy: No, I just sort of went into a shell. I just feel myself coming out of it now. I didn't cultivate any friendships. If the friends I had didn't make an effort to maintain a relationship, I let them die on the vine because I have been in a shell . . . Even at work, if I go in the coffee room and there are people there, I leave—and I have always been sort of an outgoing person. But it seems that over the past year I have sort of avoided people. I have just been coming out of it this past month. I haven't been able to involve myself in PWP or the church single group.

Of the six family types, Fragile Bond families displayed the least complicated, most straightforward approach to custody. These families had adhered to traditional sex roles. Without discussion or argument, they gave the mother custodial responsibilities at the time of separation.

Some men acknowledged they were not as child-oriented or close to their children as their wives were. They believed it would be difficult to combine child rearing with their careers and were not quite sure how they would manage the children if they had them. Like Roger, they summed up their thinking by stating that they wanted the best for their children and the best was the mother's care:

Interviewer: Did you ever consider trying to get custody?
Roger: Yeah, I thought about it, but then I didn't know what I would do with it if I got it.

Interviewer: What do you mean by that?

Roger: Well, I just didn't know. I would have to get a
                  housekeeper, and I felt that the best thing for
                  the children would be their mother. I don't think
                  the housekeeper would have the love for them
                  their mother has . . . Basically, if you love your
                  children, you get what is best for them, and I
                  really think that is best—their mother. The rest
                  of it is sort of pride, I guess, wanting them for
                  myself and not for what is going to happen to
                  them.

In all six families, both the men and women agreed that
the "best" care would be the mother's care; these families, therefore, did not dispute custody of the children.

Fractured Families

Like couples in the Fragile Bond pattern, Fractured Families were traditional in their approach to marriage. Men developed careers in engineering, law, and sales, and women remained at home, at least during the major part of their married
life. As in the Fragile Bond marriages, this traditional division of
work created a gap between husband and wife. Successful experiences outside the family increased the man's status relative
to his wife, who did not have these or other experiences to
maintain her self-esteem and high status. His work and friendships outside the home also contributed to satisfaction of some
of his needs and made him less dependent on his wife. However,
she became increasingly dependent on him as she became isolated within the home.

Fragile Bond and Fractured Families started their marriages with a similar set of assumptions about appropriate roles,
but over the course of their married life, they responded very
differently to these conditions. Fragile Bond couples separated
themselves from each other and created two different worlds:
male and female. Their marriages appeared quite conventional
and subdued as both partners preferred retreating and separat-

ing to confronting. Fractured Families did not separate but became locked into a pattern of avoidance, appeal, and attack, which escalated in intensity as the marriage progressed. Husbands tended to withdraw from their wives, and wives responded with appeals for attention and affection. These appeals stimulated more distancing behaviors in the husband; as he became more sullen and cold, the wife became more desperate and emotional in her demands.

Ann's and Ben's descriptions of their marriages illustrate the interactions of Fractured Families:

Ann: I was very much in love with him. *Extremely* proud of him, and I am to this day. I hate to say that . . . I don't know if he ever loved me . . . I would just want to talk, and he never did. I would just want him to hold me, and he couldn't be bothered. I would lay in bed and cry, and he could not understand why I was crying. He would never put his arm around me and say, "It's all right." He would just turn his back to me and go to sleep and get up and go to work.

Ann had difficulty telling the story of her marriage. She was visibly distressed and spoke with a quiet, intense voice. Frequently her voice dropped so low that her words became inaudible. Occasionally she cried and stopped talking to regain composure.

In looking back on her marriage, Ann felt she cared *too much* for her husband, Jim, but she wasn't sure he loved her. She acknowledged she had been afraid of him; she feared his withdrawal and hostile attacks.

As Ben told his story, his voice betrayed the bitterness and anger he felt toward his wife, Sally; he felt his wife had never really grown up. He was bewildered by her depressions and use of drugs and resented her need for therapy. He did not seek therapy and defined her immaturity as the primary problem in the marriage.

Difficulties appeared fairly early in these marriages, but the couples stayed together. By the time they finally separated, they had experienced some traumatic events. In some homes, anger culminated in violent attacks; for some women, depression and withdrawal resulted in excessive use of drugs and alcohol and hospitalization. These families are appropriately designated as Fractured, for their destructive interactions severed family relationships. Hostility, originally expressed in the husband/wife relationship, eventually permeated and crippled the parent/child relationship. Intense emotional distress within the home contributed to emotional problems for some children. Their social relationships and academic performance deteriorated as they were drawn into the escalating marital battle. Families were fractured, not by the divorce itself but by the destructive interactions displayed over an extensive period within the family's history.

Early Family Life: A Loss of Status. These ten women began their marriages with a romantic love relationship. They were proud of their husbands and praised them for their achievements. Each was anxious to receive her husband's approval and postured herself in favorable ways to gain his attention. She accorded him high status and accommodated and deferred to his wishes, often allowing him to make decisions for the family. Cynthia recalled:

Cynthia: It seems to me that I was very dependent upon him for any opinion that I might have. It had to come from him first. If he said we should decorate the house a certain way, I would go along with it. I would defer to him on all things.

Husbands, however, did not reciprocate in ways satisfying to their wives. Like the men in the Fragile Bond pattern, they were minimally involved with the home and the family from the beginning. They separated themselves from the home and avoided closeness with their wives. In fact, they moved against their wives and attacked them verbally and sometimes physically. Early in the relationship, however, their anger was concealed, and their wives were unable to read their husbands' feelings.

In the interviews, men reported incidents of *passive nega-tion* in which they silently criticized their wives' behaviors but did not voice these criticisms. Some men did not like their wives' methods of child rearing. Ken, for example, told this story:

Interviewer:	Did you have different philosophies on child rearing?
Ken:	Yes, but it was never explicit. There are some ways she handled things that I didn't particular-ly like, but I let them slide by. I felt that it would have as much effect on the children . . . if I brought it up.
Interviewer:	Did you feel there would be a lot of fighting if you brought it up?
Ken:	Yes.
Interviewer:	Can you think of any examples of ways in which she would deal with children that you didn't agree with?
Ken:	She set up a money pot with chores written on pieces of paper. They chose certain things and got money. I absolutely hated that. I think they should have a straight allowance but tell them to do certain things. They wouldn't have to do these things to get the allowance. They are obli-gated to do certain things around the house . . . Make them a responsible member of the family instead of a paid servant.

Other men blamed their wives for becoming pregnant. They suspected their wives had deceived them by not using con-traception. Like Harry, they did not voice these accusations:

Interviewer:	Were you using some form of contraception?
Harry:	Yes. It was effective as long as it was used. I have the suspicion that she stopped using it on pur-pose.
Interviewer:	Did you ever confront her with that?

Harry: No, what's done is done. What would be the purpose of that?

Harry, like other men in these families, began to lose some of his ideal images of his wife, Jennifer. He noticed behaviors he didn't like and silently began to devalue her. However, he did not discuss these observations with her. By avoiding any discussion of these problem areas, he did not give his wife an opportunity to change behaviors, and together, as a couple, they did not work out a compromise solution.

Some women did become aware of another form of silent hostility, a *latent anger,* which did not focus on one specific problem but consisted in a broad, pervasive hostility. Betty described her husband's anger as a reservoir that kept overflowing into all areas of life. He was constantly angry with her:

Interviewer: What was the chief problem in your marriage?
Betty: Chris's anger. He would just get fitfully angry over little things, where I'm the type it's anything to avoid an argument. I will say I'm sorry, even if I didn't do it. I remember worrying, "If I don't get this done by the time Chris gets home, he will be mad." It just seemed he was always getting mad, over little things like the sheets coming out of the water bed . . . He would call me at work and be mad about something. I would get embarrassed. You can't sit there at work and argue, right? I didn't want anybody to know what was going on, so I would hang up. He would call back two or three times. And I would get embarrassed, so pretty soon I started making jokes about it. "Well, Chris is on the line." . . . He knew he had me backed into a corner. He would be sitting here yelling and I wanted to yell back.

Some women reported that their husbands were never violent or abusive toward them, but they were aware of a latent

anger that they feared could explode into violence. After dis-
covering some sadistic pornographic pictures, Martha became
afraid of her husband's preoccupation with violence:

Martha: He had a preoccupation with violence. He used to set
             the alarm to get up and watch the horror shows on
             TV. He used to love to read books that dealt with vio-
             lent sexual crimes. Toward the end of our marriage I
             began to feel I hadn't known him at all. There was a
             level that could sometimes erupt. I started feeling just
             a little frightened of him.

Anger among the men included both a general hostility
and the criticism of a specific behavior. They were hostile
toward and critical of their own wives, but, in addition, some
men's behavior suggested they didn't like or respect women in
general.

Thus, early in the relationship, the women suffered some
loss of status. This loss was painful and was experienced as a
deprivation. They felt a reduction in emotional support; their
husbands were less attentive to their needs.

At the same time that they lost status within the relationship and in the social world, these women were becoming increasingly dependent on their husbands for support. Their need
for support intensified as they were isolated in the home with
small children. One problem shared by most of the couples was
the failure to plan a family. Seven of the ten women had unplanned children. In four families an unplanned child conceived
before marriage precipitated the marriage and disrupted plans
for school and work. In five families, the children continued to
arrive, with little space between them, resulting in large families
in a relatively short period of time.

Feeling isolated and overburdened by child care responsibilities, women began to pressure their husbands to increase
their commitments to the family. They wanted more help with
the children and more emotional support for themselves. At
first, they complained mildly. When the husbands did not re-

spond, their demands grew stronger. Finally they could not hold in their feelings of fear, anxiety, and anger, usually displayed in crying and depression.

Heavy parenting responsibilities and the wife's isolation, combined with the husband's lack of involvement, were particularly evident in one marriage. Before the ages of twenty and twenty-three, Sally and Ben had three infants under age two (a set of twins and a single baby). Ben described the impact of these infants on him and his wife:

Interviewer: What effect did they have upon Sally?
Ben: It made a raving idiot of her [laughs]. She was growing up too fast. It made her grow up too fast.
Interviewer: Did she get angry or depressed?
Ben: She got angry and depressed. She was up and down, up and down. She'd be screaming all the time. I would get off work in the early afternoon, and the door would be open. I would hear this screaming and hollering coming out, so I just kept going. I spent a lot of time in the sporting goods department at Montgomery Ward's . . . I would always try to find something to do away from the home because it was a constant hassle, this shouting and carrying on . . . I had friends. I enjoyed hunting and fishing and enjoyed the outdoors very much. I had a few friends who were single . . . and were leading single men's lives. It was kind of hard buckling down to responsibility in marriage and having a family whereas the rest of the guys were going around footloose and fancy free.

Ann described a sequence of behaviors that typified the escalating pattern of behaviors within these marriages. As her husband moved away from her, Ann renewed her efforts to retain verbal and physical contact:

Ann: I would just want to talk, and he never did. I would just
           want him to hold me, and he couldn't be bothered.

When Jim refused to respond, Ann's gestures became
more desperate. She became very frustrated and frightened:

Interviewer: How did you respond to his withdrawal?
Ann: It frightened me. That's probably where my de-
                  pression started. . . . I would lay in bed and cry,
                  and he could not understand why I was crying.

Jim responded to these *emotional displays* with an increase in avoidance. He turned away from her:

Ann: He would never put his arm around me and say, "It's all
           right." He would just turn his back to me and go to
           sleep and get up and go to work.

The couple had thus begun an escalating pattern in which the
husband's partly concealed hostility and withdrawal aroused
anxiety in his wife. Her appeals were not successful; possibly
the husband felt his wife's appeals placed upon him an obligation to reciprocate a love he did not feel. He resented her demands and withdrew from her.

Falling Out of Love: The Use of Coercive Power. As the
marriage deteriorated, both men and women used more coercive
power in their attempts to control the relationship. Women,
fearing their husbands were falling out of love with them, appealed to their husbands' commitment to the marriage and attempted to coerce responses from them. Men became more
hostile and punished their wives with threats, verbal criticisms,
displays of anger, and physical assault.

Anger, previously concealed, was displayed more openly.
Physical attacks were not always directed against the partner.
Quite often they were directed against objects within the environment or other persons. For example, the enraged husband
struck the wall, threw a dish, or put a fist through the door. The
value of such displays was really not in the actual destruction. He

did little physical damage and did not harm his wife. However, he communicated a very powerful message to his wife; his displays of aggressiveness aroused fear in her. They suggested he had reached a tolerance limit: If she pushed him beyond this limit, she risked an attack directed against her. These displays ended arguments very effectively. She knew this was the time to keep her mouth shut. Cynthia expressed her fear of these displays of verbal and physical aggressiveness:

Interviewer: Did you ever feel afraid of your husband's potential use of physical force?

Cynthia: It was frightening when Kevin was having sleeping problems between the ages of two and two and a half. Kevin would wake up and I would go in and he'd be having a bad nightmare, so I would try to wake him up. And Matt would come stomping in and grab Kevin out of my arms, and Kevin would start screaming. It was awful. I would kind of grab Kevin back and he would still be screaming. That was awful. *That* frightened me.

Interviewer: What was he going to do with Kevin?

Cynthia: I don't know. He was just grabbing. He was angry with him and probably was angry with me, for getting up with Kevin. He would say, "Just let him cry it out." I tried to explain to him that the reason I got up was so that Kevin wouldn't wake him up.

Betty had experienced violence in childhood. She wanted to protect her children from that kind of experience:

Interviewer: Weren't you afraid that when he became angry, he would become violent?

Betty: He did a couple times. I guess coming from a violent background, I could forgive it more easily. Although that was a personal goal that I had—I remembered times when I cringed in my closet

when my parents fought. I wasn't going to have
that happen for my children. It happened three or
five times in five, six years of marriage. So I
could let it happen and that was it. It wasn't
going to happen again . . . Violence wasn't that
big a factor because I was determined it wasn't
going to be.

In several marriages the violence was limited to these displays of anger, but in four marriages the violence extended to
physical assault of the wives. However, a peculiar social-psycho-
logical conspiracy evolved: Both men and women denied the
potential or real impact of violence. This denial took several
forms. First, both partners minimized the behavior. Harry said,
"I just slapped her once." Gaye recalled, "He just pushed me
against the wall." The language used suggests they discounted
the behavior. They did not see it as unusual or as creating problems.

Some women claimed they felt no fear of their husbands
when they behaved aggressively. Others admitted fear but protected their husbands by minimizing the violence, saying it was
infrequent and not hurtful.

The four women who experienced physical attacks acknowledged that they felt physical pain and admitted to a fear
of the continued use of force. However, two women continued
to legitimize the behavior and maintained their husbands were
"not violent." Instead of placing any responsibility on their
husband for the attack, they assumed responsibility. They were
attacked because they deserved it. One can imagine how desperate these women were if they had to go to the extreme of assuming responsibility for physical abuse. Denise recalled an incident in which her teenage son left the house at night. When he
didn't return as expected, she awakened her husband. Jack was
enraged at having his sleep interrupted:

Denise: That night I got hit by Jack; it was because I
                 wanted him to come with me and go look for
                 him [son] . . . He hit me twice. Now, he'd hit me

	where you wouldn't see it, on my head or maybe here, somewhere where it wouldn't show, but I remember two times on the head; I don't remember when the other time was, but I remember getting hurt so badly on my head. A couple times. But he really wasn't a violent man; I really deserved it both those times. I don't remember what the other time was, but I do know when it ended, I didn't hate him for it because I felt I deserved it . . .
Interviewer:	How many times in your marriage would you say that your husband slapped you or threatened you?
Denise:	Maybe it was more than a couple of times, but it wasn't much, really.
Interviewer:	Were you afraid at all?
Denise:	I was afraid of him hitting me, because it hurt when he hit.

Displays of anger directed toward objects, other persons, or the partner had a powerful impact on the relationship. They imposed limits on the interaction and forced the partner into compliance. Furthermore, if the woman was willing to assume blame for provoking the attack and responsibility for preventing further attacks, the problem became defined as "her" problem, not "his" problem. The problem was defined not as a problem of violence but as a problem of management, with the wife assuming responsibility for its solution.

A Bitter Ending. By the end of these marriages, these couples were recognized as troubled by community agencies. Nine of the ten couples received counseling. Five women were using alcohol and drugs excessively or had been in hospitals for treatment of depression and mental illness. The remaining five, though not identified as ill, showed signs of great emotional distress.

For some women, a retreat to drugs and alcohol came gradually as they perceived their husbands exhibiting hostile behavior and moving away from them emotionally. For Sally, a geographical move symbolized the emotional distancing and precipitated the use of drugs and alcohol. She and her husband, Ben, considered moving from their home in the urban area to a small rural community 100 miles away. He was interested in leaving his job and finding a new job with less pressure. Consequently, they moved the family to the new location. However, he subsequently changed his mind about quitting his job and relocating. He stayed in the city and commuted to the rural area to be with his family on weekends only. Ben realized he was emotionally distancing himself from his family:

Interviewer: Did the whole family move?
Ben: Yes, the whole family moved. You see, I was more or less on and off at that time about losing my job. And I wanted to move away from this area. We wanted to go out on our own. I felt more free. I do believe now it was a cover-up for emotions also.
Interviewer: A cover-up for emotions?
Ben: Yes, a cover-up. I wanted to shelve her up there. I didn't want any more hassle and baloney with her or the family. I wanted to find a period of time for myself to find out what I really wanted. It had been going on for so long I just plain had enough.

Ben enjoyed his weeks free of family hassles and decided he would not move with his family. After he turned down several job offers in the new location, Sally realized his intentions:

Ben: She knew right there and then that I shelved her when I turned the job down. That was the beginning of the end for the marriage. She knew she was shelved.

She responded with anger and began seeking other men, alcohol, and drugs:

Ben: She started going out with men and started going to different bars. She loved drinking, and if she wasn't drinking, she was taking Valium. Anything to escape.

Ann recalled the final months of her marriage—a time that had ended with her voluntary hospitalization for treatment of depression. She and her husband, Jim, had decided to try a separation, as they felt the stress of their marriage increasing.

During the separation, the relationship appeared to become more enjoyable for both of them. One day Jim made a unilateral decision to return and moved his things back into the house while Ann was gone. Their relationship deteriorated in the days and weeks after he returned:

Ann: When he came home, we never discussed our problems or what was going on. He just moved in and we carried on our lives, but yet he never talked to me and he never put his arm around me. The whole year he was home we had no sexual relations whatsoever. He came home but never touched me once . . . There never was any handholding or fondling or cuddling.

Interviewer: You never just hugged each other in bed or anything like that?

Ann: No, never. Never even during the day. I would want to put my arms around him in the kitchen and hug, and he would say, "Just go away."

As Jim increasingly avoided Ann, she became very depressed. She sought the help of her family physician, who prescribed medication, and eventually felt compelled to submit herself to a hospital. The intensity of her depressions frightened her:

Interviewer: Why did you commit yourself to the hospital?

Ann: For the depression. I cried and I slept a lot. The marriage was over, and I couldn't face that.

Conflict and Competition in Parenting. The most salient characteristic of the Fractured Families was the woman's loss of status and power. Over a period of time in the marriage, women lost efficacy as wives, mothers, and persons in the community, while men achieved social and professional success. Prolonged stress, a destructive marital relationship, and a lack of alternative resources outside the marriage contributed to this loss of status and power.

Heavy parenting responsibilities and a deteriorating marriage created stress for the women. Since they remained within the home, they did not have the support of outside employment or social networks. They were, therefore, vulnerable to their husbands' avoidance and hostility. The combination of little support within the marriage and limited resources outside it gradually eroded their confidence in themselves as wives and as human beings.

By the end of the marriage, the women lacked not only self-confidence but also real effectiveness in their actual social relationships. Their ineffectiveness and loss of power were revealed in three areas: management and control of the children, their marital relationship, and management of their public image.

First, several of these mothers had a great deal of difficulty managing their children, particularly male children. This problem was presented in various ways in different families. In three families, mothers had difficulty managing their school-age boys. These boys were abusive toward them and refused to follow their rules. In two other families, Gaye and Susan lost viability as parents when their husbands and teenage sons formed coalitions against them. In the history of these two families, each parent had tried to win the favor and support of the children. Both parents in these families were authoritarian. Communication and interaction among family members were limited. The parents did not support each other's disciplinary actions. Over a period of time, the children formed a coalition with one parent. This coalition may have shifted back and forth between the parents as the children were growing up, but by the time the boys became teenagers, they were quite firmly identified with their father. Gaye and Susan felt frustrated in their efforts to discipline their sons and were bothered by signs of growing disrespect.

In addition to losing control over their children, women also lost efficacy in their relationship with their husbands. They were fearful of both the psychological and physical damage the husband could inflict on them. They were vulnerable to his hostility and did not develop effective strategies for coping with his aggressiveness. Denise and Joan, for example, yielded custody when threatened by their husbands. Ken had learned the power of an open-ended threat and let it be known that if he didn't get the children, he would take them from the area. He did not specify where he would go, but he obtained passports for himself and the children. How much information he actually gave her about his plans is unclear. Although Joan wanted the children, she realized that if she did gain custody, he would possibly leave the country with the children. Thus, he successfully blocked her efforts by the use of a threat. She indicated she wanted the children but was fearful about pressing too hard for custody.

Finally, women lost credibility as responsible, effective adults. One woman had become addicted to drugs and alcohol. Four others had received extensive psychological counseling; two of these women had voluntarily entered a hospital for a brief period to receive help. One woman was committed three more times by her husband and therapist when they judged she needed help. These women, therefore, were labeled as mentally ill or alcoholic, by community agencies and by professionals as well as by their families.

When it came to contesting custody, some women were inept in managing the legal battle. Seven women had a great deal of difficulty presenting themselves favorably during the dissolution proceedings. They were not able to control their emotions in their interviews with lawyers, social workers, psychologists, and judges. They were depressed and angry, and their tearful incoherence was a sharp contrast to their husbands' much more calm, coherent, and forceful demeanor. To the professionals who had to determine which parent would be more effective for the child, these differences in presentation of self must have been dramatic.

Women also had difficulty organizing legal support for themselves. They did not plan adequately and were always at least two steps behind their husbands, who prepared carefully and well for a legal battle for custody. They were slower in contacting a lawyer. Furthermore, they were not especially selective in their choice of lawyers. They placed confidence in lawyers recommended by friends or relatives without first ascertaining the lawyer's capabilities in assuming a custody case. They left the legal battle to the attorney, which, unfortunately, often resulted in an ineffective legal performance. Lawyers, who were sure their female clients would win a custody battle, prepared inadequately. In contrast, lawyers representing men were aware of the difficulties involved and tended to be more careful and thorough in their preparations.

Women did not consider getting character witnesses for themselves or employing a psychologist to test their children. Men, however, often employed these tactics. This weakness in preparing a legal case may have been prompted by a personal lack of assertiveness. Lack of knowledge about community resources and/or a preoccupation with internal stresses that incapacitated these women and made it difficult for them to act decisively may also have contributed to an inadequate legal case. Regardless of the causes, ineffectiveness in preparing a legal defense again demonstrated women's lack of power and ineffectiveness in negotiating for themselves.

All ten women either lost or relinquished custody of their children, but two regained custody. Denise regained custody of her teenage daughter when her husband declared he no longer wanted custodial responsibilities; Jennifer received custody after bringing the case back to court for a long battle. Quite clearly, these women appeared ineffectual as parents and as litigants in court. In contrast, men presented to the court and community records of stable employment and occupational success and an image of competence. They demonstrated sophistication and expertise in the organization and presentation of themselves in the courtroom. In the eyes of their children, their wives, and the community, they were more effective and powerful parents.

4

𝔑 𝔑

Women's Needs and Rights
as Catalysts for Breakup

𝔙 𝔙

The middle group of families differed in several ways from Fragile Bond and Fractured Families. These differences included age differences: They were younger, had been married for a shorter time, and had younger children. More significantly, they had developed different patterns of interaction over the course of their family history.

Eight couples followed a pattern similar to that portrayed by Ibsen in his play *A Doll's House.* These husbands were very much committed to their marriages; they loved their wives and valued family life. Like Helmer in *A Doll's House,* these men also followed a pattern that seemed natural to them. They controlled their wives. Early in the marriage, women appreciated their husbands' affections and accepted their domination, but at some point they changed. Therapy or a return to school or work enabled these women to become more assertive. Men resisted changes in their wives and conflict developed. Like Nora, these women ultimately decided the only way to retain their individual identity was to leave their Doll's House Marriage. Their husbands were stunned and overwhelmed by their wives' refusal to continue a pattern of married life that appeared natural and comfortable to them.

In another group of families in this middle group, four couples followed a different pattern. At the beginning of their marriages, they may have resembled Fragile Bond marriages, as the men were quite self-contained and not comfortable with expressing themselves emotionally. The four wives in this group, however, did not accept withdrawal. They became angry and challenged the husband's passivity. They pleaded, threatened, and sometimes even moved aggressively against their husbands, in an attempt to elicit a response. These marriages are best described as Stalemate Marriages; men and women were locked into an unproductive pattern in which the women demanded and the men retreated. The more the wives threatened, the more detached the men became. Just as in the stalemate position in chess, the partners were deadlocked in an impasse. Unable to change this stalemated position, the frustrated women eventually left the marriage.

In addition to age differences, the most notable differences between the older and middle families were the differences in women's responses. Even in marriages that began in fairly traditional patterns, women changed and demanded more from their husbands. Unlike the women in Fragile Bond marriages who accepted separation within marriage and the women in Fractured Families who became lodged in a dependent role that was ultimately destructive to them, these women struggled to change the pattern of their marriage. Undoubtedly, their employment outside the home made them feel more confident and able to survive by themselves. Perhaps it was their perception of choices and alternatives outside the marriage that enabled them to move away from marriages that no longer satisfied their needs.

Doll's House Marriages

Nancy: I was being controlled and I just didn't have a
                chance to be myself. Things were really going

downhill . . . I was just very unhappy. At that point I asked him if I could go into therapy, and he would have none of it. He said there was nothing wrong with me and I should just pull myself together. Then it got to the point, the more I brought it out, that I was the crazy one. If the marriage was falling apart, it was my fault. I just needed to get myself together . . . I remember making an appointment, not telling him, and being scared to death to tell him. Then the therapist called me at home and Greg was livid. I was working part-time and I decided, what the hell, I was going to take the money from my job and go into therapy. All the other times the money from my job had gone into a common pool. So that's what I told him . . .

Interviewer: What was his attitude while you were in therapy?

Nancy: Very threatened. I think he knew that once I got it together, I was going to leave . . . I moved out last Christmas.

Nancy married Greg as he began his medical school education. During the early years of their marriage, Greg's career was central to their marriage. His professional training and the establishment of his first practice determined their geographical location, the timing of their children, and her employment. During these early years, Nancy willingly accommodated and adapted her life around his plans; she also deferred to him as an expert in family issues. Since he had some course work and clinical experiences in pediatrics in medical school, she assumed he knew more about child rearing than she did; consequently, she followed his advice. For example, she gave up breast feeding when he indicated bottle feeding was a preferred method.

About twelve years after the marriage began, Nancy reached a crisis point. She became aware of the degree to which Greg controlled her life and made decisions for her and the children. She became very unhappy with her own life and with the marriage and knew she needed help. For perhaps the first time in a major issue, she took an action opposed by her husband: She sought therapy against his wishes. In therapy she became more sure of herself and more willing to take steps to change her situation. Eventually she initiated a separation and divorce.

Doll's House Marriages differed from marriages in other patterns in three ways: in power plays used by the husband and wife, in styles of coping with crises encountered within the marriage and in characteristics of age, length of marriage, and employment patterns.

In their marital interaction, both the men and women in these marriages expressed a strong emotional commitment to each other and to the marriage; they placed a great deal of importance on family life. During the course of their marriages, they appealed to each other's sense of commitment to the relationship. They expected loyalty and emotional responsiveness from each other.

Although both men and women appealed to each other's commitment to the marriage, they appealed to each other in very different ways. Quite typically women used appeals that implied a subordinate position in the relationship. They accepted their husbands' ideas and tried to bring their own behavior into line with those expectations. They gave priority to their husbands' wishes and gained support for their own needs primarily through requesting and appealing to their husbands.

Men, however, more frequently used appeal behaviors implying a superordinate position within the relationship. They assumed their ideas would be accepted by their wives. They expected accommodation and acted quite assertively in gaining concessions from their wives.

During the course of the marriage, however, these patterns changed as the wife either returned to school or work or entered therapy. These events served as turning points for these families. The wives' behaviors changed: They discontinued many of their subordinate appeal gestures and became much more assertive in their demands. As they changed, men escalated their demands and complaints. Eventually the women in these eight families left their marriages.

These families differed from other families in another way. They were younger than the families in the Fragile Bond and Fractured Family patterns, and the women followed a different kind of work pattern. At the time of divorce, these couples had been married an average of thirteen years; the husbands were about thirty-eight and the wives thirty-seven. Children were spread from teenage to preschool years. With twelve boys and five girls, these eight families had approximately two children each.

Similar to men in the other patterns, six men were employed in sales and business positions. One was a teacher and another was a physician. Women, however, did not remain in the traditional homemaking role and, thus, were quite different from women in the Fragile Bond and Fractured Family patterns. With the exception of one woman, they were employed for two thirds or more of their married life. Their employment followed a variety of patterns, but the most common was for the woman to be unemployed for a short time after the birth of the children; she then returned to work part-time and eventually full-time. Their occupations ranged from secretary to engineer.

Posturing, Rewarding, and Persuading. Men and women in these marriages quite typically appealed to each other through posturing, rewarding, and persuading. Posturing behaviors are attempts to present one's self favorably to gain the spouse's approval. Women used posturing behaviors more frequently than men, and they postured themselves differently than men did. At times they postured themselves to meet the demands of a specific situation. Nancy recalled the way she managed the birth of their first child:

Nancy: The birth of the child was very interesting. I can remember med students used to talk about these wommen who were shrieking and so forth in labor. I had read, I can't remember, this big thick OB book, and I was getting all primed for this. I was determined that I wasn't going to embarrass Greg, as a medical student's wife, so I didn't say a *thing*! You know, no matter what the labor was doing, I didn't do anything. I was just very calm. At one point, I asked him for

some ice chips. He looked at me, and I said, "The
book said I can have ice chips!"

Nancy became very familiar with her husband's and the medical
profession's definitions of appropriate childbearing behavior. In
an effort to accommodate to these expectations, she coached
herself on delivery behavior. She was also willing to defend her
behavior as appropriate and legitimate within the standards of
the medical profession.

Women also accommodated to more general cultural
norms that defined their roles as wives or mothers. Arlene could
allow herself the privilege of work only if she first proved herself in the primary role of mother and housekeeper:

Arlene: With the first child, we still lived in an apartment. I
            did everything without saying one word as far as
            being a mother, taking care of the house, and I never
            asked him to do one thing. This was partly because I
            wanted to do it; I wanted to show that I could be a
            mother, a worker, and everything else and not have
            one complaint. That was my big aim in life.

Men seldom postured themselves. When they did, their
posturing behaviors appeared quite different from women's.
Masculine posturing behaviors suggested attempts to manage
and shape their partner's responses rather than accommodate
to them.

Doris came from a very religious family. Before she married, Glen presented himself as dedicated to the church and religious activities. However, after the marriage, his interest in religion declined, and he admitted that he had assumed this interest
to gain approval from her and her parents. He knew the kind of
husband she was looking for, and he "played his cards right."
After he married her, he no longer needed this approval, and he
gave up the posturing behavior. He could then admit he had little interest in religion.

The couples in this group frequently used a second type
of appeal behavior—rewarding. They praised each other and ex-

pressed their affection physically and verbally. Nancy said her husband valued her femininity:

Nancy: In some ways he made it very clear to me that I was a female and that I could be desirable as a female.

Kevin reported his wife demonstrated sympathy and genuine caring:

Kevin: When I felt down, she felt genuine concern. It wasn't that there was anything she could do about it, but she was sympathetic . . . Even when things were really bad, she was there. She cared, she always cared, even though she was frustrated, she cared.

Both men and women used rewarding gestures, and there appeared to be no differences in their styles of showing affection. Men, however, used another type of behavior more than women—persuasion. They talked, admonished, and argued their wives into some course of action. Beth recalled:

Beth: We talked and talked and talked. What it ended up was that I always got talked into things, or out of things. Brian was very convincing.

Virginia and Kevin conceived a child before they felt ready to have one. Since Kevin was still in college and they had been married only a short time, they were not ready financially or emotionally to have a child. Virginia wanted to keep the child, but Kevin favored an abortion.

Kevin: We talked, but we just didn't agree. I think we talked about the abortion well over two weeks.

Interviewer: Why do you think she actually agreed to it, then?

Kevin: She saw how much I wanted it—how much or how important it was to me as I perceived our situation. I've always been stronger-willed than her. I think she got to a point where after we talked so much, she intellectualized it.

Interviewer: She could see it was the rational solution to the problem.

Kevin: But she wasn't emotionally prepared. It is really hard to go back and say what is right and what is wrong. I choose to think that everything that happened is right [laughs].

These couples thus resolved some important emotion-laden issues by a logical consideration of facts. This focus on facts tended to suppress the emotionality of the event and encouraged the wife to deny expression of her emotions. Strong emotions, submerged at the time the couple made a decision, often reappeared later, usually immediately preceding the divorce. The forcefulness of these feelings, as they emerged at a later date, surprised and confused both the husband and wife.

Status Reduction and Inflation. Posturing, rewarding, and persuading were subtle, unobtrusive behaviors built into the fiber of daily life; they did not intrude visibly into the relationship. Their full impact was usually not realized for years.

Other behaviors were not so subtle. They were more visible and intense. These behaviors intensified the distance in power positions between husband and wife. They reduced the status of one partner and raised or inflated the status of the other. Women, for example, assumed a lower position or status when they took responsibility for marital interaction and blamed themselves for family problems. In addition, they inflated their husband's status when they allowed him to assume the superior position of expert; they consulted with him, yielded to his opinions, and relied on him for decisions in every matter.

Women accommodated to their husbands' judgments and decisions, even when they had strong preferences of their own. Later they resented their husbands' expectations and their own willingness to conform. Nancy allowed her husband's expertise as a physician to influence her decision on breast feeding, a decision she later regretted.

Interviewer: What immediate effects do you feel this first baby had on you?

Nancy: It was difficult in that Greg was interested in pediatrics as a medical student. So he had definite ideas about what should be done, what should not be done. Because of that I felt under pressure to try to conform and do what "I was supposed to be doing." I wanted to breast-feed her and he did not want me to. I can particularly remember that, and I have never really forgiven him for that. But it was my fault too because I was not assertive enough at that time to be able to say what I wanted.

In addition to validating their spouses' opinions, women gave priority to men's activities. The husbands' interests and employment assumed a position of central importance within marriage. Women often reported placing aside their own career development to aid their husbands' careers. Ann Marie talked about the effects Steven's moves had on her attempts to establish herself:

Interviewer: Did he help or hinder you in your career?

Ann Marie: He was in the Air Force, and that hindered my career. Our first fight was when I was working for a computer department. They were going to train me to be a programmer. He was going off to Texas. At that time I suggested I stay here during that year to get the training. It was a good opportunity for me. He said, "No, you can get that in Texas." It turned out I worked in a department store and I never got the training. So, yes, I think he hindered my career. We were a year here and a year there.

After her husband was out of the service, he worked for a private business firm. Again, he was expected to move about

every two years. She resented the constant moves and became
frustrated with efforts to start her career:

Ann Marie:	We spent two years working to get the house fixed up, weekends, evenings. We were just about done with the kitchen, which was a huge project. And he came home one evening and said, "They want to send me to Boston." And things were really nice for me. I was very comfortable with my work situation. And I said, "I am not going anywhere." Steven's father came down and told me I should go. But I said, "I am not going." So we did talk about it, but it was apparent that when push came to shove, his advancing was more important to him.
Interviewer:	Could he understand your situation, that you had a good job?
Ann Marie:	He didn't think it was a good job. He said, "You aren't doing anything here you can't do in Boston."
Interviewer:	Was that true?
Ann Marie:	I could have done it again, but it would have meant starting over again. One of the reasons I got to the level I did was because people knew me. They knew me and recommended me to clients and said, "She is good at this and that." I could have done it, but it would have been hard to do.

Men in these families reduced their wives' status and increased their own by insisting on having their own way and expecting their wives to grant requests and comply with demands.
If there was a conflict between needs, the husband discounted
his wife's needs and insisted on doing things his own way. Demands were explicit or implicit. Explicit demands were verbal-
ized or sometimes even presented in written form. Beth, who
was teaching full-time, had just had her first child; she found

her husband intensified his expectations of her after the child was born. She said:

Beth: He had a list of things to do. He kept adding things to this list.

Interviewer: What kinds of things did he have on this list?

Beth: Well, having dinner on time and washing out his gym clothes every night. He took a class in Kung-Fu or played basketball. So I had to wash the clothes every night. And there were just a lot of errands I had to run ... I had to go to the cleaner's after work and pick up shirts for him, and the grocery store, and pick up the baby at the sitter's ... He felt that when he came home, everything should be ready.

Men also reduced their wives' status by implying their wives' activities were trivial and unimportant. Doris felt her husband never showed any interest in what she was doing:

Doris: I used to read psychology rather extensively, and he always put it down. Whereas if I had shown an interest in opera, which is something he wanted me to be interested in, then he would take an interest. I have been asking myself why people are like that, and I think people feel anxious when they are not in control.

Kevin married a woman who was very interested in establishing a home. Early in their marriage Virginia focused a great deal of time and attention on the home, which he felt was not the best use of time:

Kevin: In a way I gave her some negative reinforcement because I perhaps made her feel that being a housewife wasn't very good ... I told her she was great, but I said, "You have more to offer yourself and other people than being a housewife." I always said "housework" like "Housework! That's the pits! What are you doing in here!?"

Men also sometimes put down their wives in front of other people. They ridiculed, belittled, or harassed their wives with petty grievances and complaints. Nancy said that when her husband put her down, his behavior was imitated by a male friend:

Nancy: Greg had a definite habit of putting me down in front of people. He just delighted in that—just very subtle putdowns. It had built up during the years. Jon had this thing, whenever he was with Greg, he and Greg put Ann and me down. It got to the point where Ann refused to come up and visit us. She couldn't stand the situation any longer. And Jon always felt guilty when he left.

A Shift in Power. In the early years of these marriages, husbands established control by persuading and demanding. Wives probably felt that giving in to their husbands was preferable to creating conflict. However, over the years, the small accommodations formed a pattern. The reference point was always the husband; his definition of the situation became accepted as the norm. Several years passed before women recognized they had established a pattern, in which they were losing some of their own identity. Beth realized her loss:

Beth: Well, I got so involved with him and what he wanted. I went to the grocery store and all of a sudden I wasn't buying for me. I was buying for him, what he wanted to eat and the way he wanted it fixed. And everything was what *he* wanted. What he would like. Not whether I would like it tonight or whether I would like it for myself. I just got so wrapped up in what he wanted, and I lost a part of me somewhere.

As women recognized this pattern, they experienced a

crisis. A few sought therapy during this period; through this therapy they often formulated new perceptions and were motivated to change. When these women began therapy, they were not ready to move toward divorce. They tried to bring their husbands into therapy with them. This, however, did not prove to be fruitful for the couple. Some husbands were quite threatened by their wives' movement into therapy and used this as a device to prove their wives were the crazy or guilty parties. Nancy described her husband's response:

Interviewer: What was his attitude while you were in therapy?
Nancy: Very threatened. I think he knew that once I got it together, I was going to leave . . . I moved out last December. I really wasn't thinking about divorce then. I just wanted to get out of there.
Interviewer: Do you think therapy affected your position on divorce?
Nancy: I think so. I don't think I could have left before that. I had the feeling of tremendous guilt.
Interviewer: Guilt for what?
Nancy: For feeling that I wanted out, for giving up. I tried and tried and tried. There must be something wrong with me . . . I was the crazy one.

Not all crises were stimulated by a heightened personal awareness, however. Two very common types of crises arose from changes in the family arrangements. For at least six of the eight marriages, the first critical period appeared immediately following the birth of either the first or last child. Women in these families experienced the birth of the first child as stressful. They resented the isolation imposed on them. Finding it very difficult to arrange any kind of life for themselves outside the home, they missed the freedom they had experienced before the birth of the child. They were tense and anxious about the child's behavior.

Soon after the birth of the first or second child, the women returned to work. Their return to work created another crisis for these families. Even though husbands in many cases encouraged their wives' employment, they found it difficult to cope with the consequences of that employment. They resented their wives' demands for increased participation in housework, not just because it involved more work for them but because it signified a new assertiveness in their wives. Kevin felt that his wife's return to work made her more demanding:

Interviewer: How did you feel about her work?

Kevin: I was glad that she got the job. I thought that it would kind of help her, because she had begun to indicate dissatisfaction with sitting around and not doing anything. She wanted the job, and so she got it, and we were both happy about it. But almost immediately she started showing this change of personality and that I didn't like, so then the job itself became kind of an issue... All of a sudden she got this real independent attitude. Finally she was making some money on her own, and there was a *definite* change as soon as she started working.

Interviewer: How did you perceive this change?

Kevin: Mostly it was just negativity directed at me. It reminded me of the way children rebel sometimes against a little bit of authority. On some of those things where maybe she had been doing the majority of the housework, all of a sudden she was telling me that I was going to have to do this and that and the other thing because she was now making money, even though she was making only one fourth of what I made. But she was all of a sudden demanding that I do half the housework ... It wasn't so much the housework. I didn't really mind that. It was more that she felt her own importance all of a sudden.

Men also realized their wives were changing in their relationships with other people. With an expanding social and work life, women were meeting attractive men. Thoughts of potential lovers disturbed the husbands.

At the same time that the marriage relationship was deteriorating, men were experiencing problems with employment. Three of the eight men in this group became very dissatisfied with their jobs. They either quit or lost several jobs during the final years of the marriage. A fourth man worked part-time while he went to school. His job meant very little to him; he was marking time until he could qualify for another job. Another man retired after twenty years in the military service. He tried retirement but didn't like the inactivity and found another full-time job. Of the eight men, only three were happy with their work and had careers to which they were committed. The rest were experiencing change and turmoil related to their work. The husband's often painful reassessment of his own work coincided with his wife's enthusiasm for a new career. As he faced his fears of failure, he was doubly threatened by her new successes.

As men experienced increasing insecurity on the job and decreasing satisfaction in the marriage, they became angry and frustrated. They became depressed; some expressed their anger in threats of violence against themselves and others around them. Through these threats, the man sometimes appeared to his wife as a victim. Arlene felt her husband assumed this role:

Arlene: Michael became a victim, many, many times with his job; someone either didn't understand him or didn't like him and he didn't get the promotion . . . He couldn't be productive on the job at all. He got more and more depressed . . . He was threatening suicide at the time. I went to my girlfriend's house and stayed with her. The next day he called and told my friend, "I guess I overplayed my hand, I couldn't get Arlene to listen to me." It wasn't really like a charade because he was too capable of getting into it, but the whole point was that he was trying to get my attention.

Both Arlene and Michael recognized he was trying to manipulate her, but his threats frightened her. Demands phrased in more subtle language earlier in the marriage now erupted in the strident language of violence. In another family, Glen, who had not been physically abusive toward his wife or children during the marriage, forced entry into Doris's home and threatened to shoot the entire family as well as himself. Fortunately, since these men did not appear to have a history of violence, one abortive attempt was usually sufficient to restore their perspective. Embarrassed by behavior that was so foreign to their usual style, they ruefully retreated and expressed their distress less violently.

Men and women in this pattern did not respond similarly to the divorce. Men appeared to be much more distressed with the end of the marriage than women. They more frequently reported feeling depressed and lonely. Some indicated they were not meeting or dating women. Three men were also not secure financially; they were either unemployed or just beginning to establish their own businesses.

In contrast, women in this group viewed their divorce as difficult but growth-producing. They were enthusiastic about their newly developing or continuing careers; they were excited about new experiences and activities. They had met men and were experimenting with new relationships. Although some were still involved in disputes with their husbands over child care or finances, they tended to speak of their marriage as a thing of the past; they focused on the present and future rather than the past.

At the time of divorce, these eight families showed very diverse responses to the issue of custody. Beth and Brian's response was very similar to responses of Fragile Bond families. Brian was less involved with the child, and they both simply assumed he would remain with Beth. Virginia and Kevin shared their child, much like couples in the Perfect Model marriages. Another two couples were similar to Stalemate families, in which the mother gradually phased out her involvement with the children and ultimately left them with their father. Ann Marie and Sue followed this pattern. In a fifth family, the mother retained custody but neither parent was fully involved with or attentive to the children's needs.

The remaining three families demonstrated a unique pattern not present in any of the other families. Children in these families blamed the mother for the divorce and saw their father as the victim, the loser. These children assumed a protective role as Caretaker for their fathers. At least temporarily, roles were reversed as children behaved in a parental, supportive way and fathers depended on their children for support. Age and sex affected the children's perceptions of their fathers and their ability to manage this caretaking role.

Stalemate Marriages

Vic: I never was really a real emotional person, you know. I kind of roll with the punches, right? I'm still that way, I think, although I'm beginning to get more concerned about things as I grow older ... I figure I make my own breaks and what happens in my life *I* have control of. And I don't worry so much about other people and what they do or what they say or what they don't do ...

Interviewer: What about a family situation? Were you more concerned if your kids or wife were doing something you didn't like?

Vic: No, no.

Vic portrayed himself as a strong individualist with little need for emotional expressiveness. Although he enjoyed physical affection, he found it hard to talk about or express his feelings. Furthermore, he believed there was little value in such expressions. He did not wish to become too closely involved with those around him. He reasoned that each person alone is responsible for his behavior. He insisted that other people's behavior did not affect him, and he tended to dismiss their actions with a shrug of his shoulders. Thus, he projected the image that nothing ever really bothered or affected him. Life, he had found, was much easier if he accepted whatever came his way and simply "rolled with the punches."

His wife, Maria, often complained to him about their lack

of communication. She resented his separateness and his refusal to take her concerns seriously. His passive shrug of the shoulder irritated and angered her. When her appeals, complaints, and frustrated outbursts failed to get a response, she gave up on the marriage and walked away. He made no attempt to delay or stop her and steadfastly maintained that she had a right to leave if she was unhappy. Being quite pragmatic, he directed his attention and energies to resolving issues of child care and maintenance of the household.

Men and women in the Stalemate Marriages differed from men and women in the other family patterns in their style of interaction. Their age and stage in the family life cycle, approach to marital roles, and experiences with parenting also differentiated them from other families.

Men in the Stalemate Marriages were most similar to men in the Fragile Bond families. Like them, they tended to avoid expressing strong emotions. They were particularly uncomfortable with anger and steadfastly refused to admit to being irritated, annoyed, or upset. But they were also different from men in the Fragile Bond families. The degree to which they withdrew was greater; three of the four also tended to withhold sexually as well as emotionally. And unlike men in the Fragile Bond families who made some demands on their wives and gave them some attention, these men neither invited nor demanded responses from their wives.

The women in this group were very different from women in the Fragile Bond families. Whether their differences emerged from the husband's more extended withdrawal or from their own more contemporary views of marriage, these women tended to be much more demanding than women in the Fragile Bond families. They did not allow their husbands' withdrawal to go unnoticed or unchallenged. They were angry with their husbands, and they cajoled, pleaded, criticized, complained, and finally verbally and physically threatened them. As they moved more aggressively, however, the men retreated and became even less responsive. Like Maria, these women ended the marriage when they recognized they could not elicit a response from their husbands.

These men and women were also younger than the couples in the Fragile Bond, Fractured Families, or Doll's House Marriages. They were all in their thirties, with thirty-six the average age for men and thirty-four for women. They had been married an average of ten years. Only one family had a young teenager; the other children were school age. Six of their seven children were boys.

Men in this group were employed in business, teaching, and entertainment. Women were employed as a clerk, office manager, and dental technician. One woman was completing her doctorate at a university.

Although they did not have the positions of status and responsibility that some women in other family patterns had, these women were striving for advancement. They were not content with their mothering and homemaking roles. To some degree, they viewed their mothering responsibilities as conflicting with their own development. For all four women, childbearing and child rearing had been stressful. Sandra and Maria both conceived their first child before marriage, when they were eighteen and nineteen. Sandra was very depressed during the pregnancy because the forced marriage and birth interfered with her plans to move back east and attend school. Her husband, Gary, realized she was despondent with changes in her plans and acknowledged that the child's arrival did not interfere with his schooling or career plans. He insisted that Sandra care for the infant and refused to take responsibility for his physical care.

Sandra had no more children, but Maria had a total of four children within six years. When questioned about the impact of these closely spaced children on his wife, Vic responded that he didn't think they created any problems for Maria.

The third couple, Joyce and Dan, planned to adopt a child and then have one of their own later. After they adopted a boy, Joyce decided she didn't want any more children; she was in graduate school preparing for an academic career. She felt children would restrict her too much. Dan was very upset by her refusal to have children, as he very much wanted a child of his own. In another family, Velma and Fred agreed on two children and had two boys. The younger boy was tragically killed in an auto accident, and the family was grief-stricken. Although both Velma and Fred suffered, they were not able to share their distress or comfort each other. The loss of the child, therefore, underscored the estrangement already existing between them. Thus, in each of these four families, some emotional distress was associated with either planning or raising children.

Withholding and Demanding. Men in these marriages realized they withheld themselves emotionally from their wives. They also recognized the difficulties they had in confronting and showing anger. Dan said he internalized his anger and allowed it to build up until he could contain it no longer. Then he "let loose," and the relationship, as far as he was concerned, was over. Other men never "let loose" and maintained a stoic posture even after their wives left them.

Men gave different explanations for their avoidance behaviors. Vic, for example, incorporated uninvolvement into his philosophy of life. He believed people should be responsible for their own behaviors and should not be influenced or controlled by others in their choices. Even when Maria began to date other men toward the end of their marriage, Vic maintained the attitude "If that's something she wants to do, she should do it."

Gary did not connect his separateness with an ideological stance of individualism and self-responsibility. Rather, he perceived his withholding as a strategy to avoid *self*-confrontation. He was denying a reality to himself, a reality that, if faced, would require decisions and changes. And he feared those changes:

Gary: I avoided in my marriage telling Sandra how I felt because I knew that if I ever admitted it, it would mean admitting it to myself. And if I ever admitted it to myself, the marriage would have to end. My role would end; I would no longer be a husband. I would be a man without a woman, and I would have to fill up my life somehow. I would have to find someone. I would have to go out, and I would have to face my own loneliness. I was lonely all the time I was married. I've been lonely all my life. I've been a-*lone.* I've done all kinds of things to fill that up. And I'm so grateful to Sandra for leaving me because she forced me to face myself and find out who I really was.

Gary also felt he used withholding behavior to punish his wife. He could not show his hostility toward Sandra directly, but he could show it indirectly by refusing to give her the responses she wanted. For example, on weekends, he spent a great deal of time with his painting hobby:

Gary: She would walk back and forth while I was painting and didn't pay the least bit of attention to it. And so I wouldn't pay any attention to her. I can remember sometimes her coming down, and I would be here and the painting would be there, and she would stand in front of it and *scream* at me: *Why* wasn't I paying attention to her? Why was the painting more important than she was? And I did my [pause] what I have sensed was a passive-aggressive number; I just would not respond to her. I would just go on, hoping she would scream herself out, and, of course, that was more provoking than ever.

The husbands' refusals to respond triggered angry outbursts from the wives. Most of the time these displays of anger were limited to verbal abuses and threats, but occasionally they erupted into more open displays of physical anger. Velma recalled how she occasionally threw something at Fred or hit him. She recounted a conversation she had with him toward the end of the marriage after she discovered he had a relationship with another woman:

Velma: What is going on between you and this girl?
Fred: [Shocked tone] How can you say something like that?
Velma: Oh, Jesus! [Hits him with hand] I have seen my lawyer and I am filing for a divorce!
Fred: [Expressionless tone] Oh.

Velma:	Yes, I think it's time you left home.
Fred:	Oh.
Velma:	Do you have anything to say?
Fred:	No.
Velma:	I just asked you to get out of my house after fourteen years! [Agitated voice] What do you want to know?
Fred:	Can I see John once in a while?
Velma:	Yes, anything you want. [Angrily] What do you want?
Fred:	[No response.]

As Velma recounted this conversation, she used an angry, forceful voice for her remarks and a weak, inexpressive, barely audible voice for Fred's responses. Quite possibly, Velma really did not want to end the marriage but was desperately attempting to find an issue shocking enough to engage him in interaction. She was stunned and angry when even the demand to leave the house failed to elicit a response.

Joyce was more aggressive than the other women. Immediately before the separation, she threatened Dan with a knife. Dan described these experiences:

Interviewer:	Was there any violence in the marriage?
Dan:	Actually there was violence on her part. Threatening, walking around with a knife, waving it, threatening me. I moved out for a day because she threatened to kill me in my sleep.

In each of these four marriages, the women initiated the final breakup of the marriage by either leaving the house themselves or forcing their husbands to leave. Both Sandra and Maria left their children as well as husbands. Gary and Vic were content to have the children remain with them and felt that it was a reasonable decision. From the beginning they believed their wives were not comfortable with the children. They felt they were awkward in caring for them, did not hold them much, and were not physically affectionate. With time, Sandra and Maria became even less involved with and more separated from the children.

Although Gary and Vic had not assumed much responsibility for the infants, they had become more involved with the children as they grew. By the time their wives left the marriage, they had developed a companionship with their children. It thus seemed natural to them that the children should remain in the home with them after their wives left.

When Joyce and Dan separated, they both assumed she would retain custody of their child, Michael. However, they changed their plans after conferring with the child's psychiatrist. He felt it would be in the child's best interests to remain with his father. Dan had an established occupational position, but Joyce was preparing to undertake doctoral research in a foreign country. The psychiatrist reasoned the father could provide more security and stability for Michael. In addition, he expressed concern for the child's fear of the mother. In his judgment, Joyce's aggressive outbursts disturbed Michael. Family members also encouraged Joyce to give custody to Dan; they convinced her that caring for a child and maintaining a house would add considerably to her other responsibilities as a graduate student and teacher.

In the fourth family, Velma retained custody. She perceived Fred's relationship with the child as rather distant. When they separated, neither of them appeared to even consider the issue of custody; both assumed Velma would keep the child.

5

Unrealistic Demands
and Expectations
in Contemporary Marriages

The younger families followed two patterns, which were very different from each other. Eight families in the first pattern appeared as ideal contemporary marriages. These men and women were successful in many dimensions of life. Men, in particular, were highly educated and successful in their careers. Several of the women in this group were also well educated and had careers that they valued. Marital interactions appeared versatile and flexible, as these couples managed to avoid the stereotyped roles and deadlocked positions characteristic of other family patterns. Healthy children were progressing well in school and were a credit to their parents' abilities in child rearing. Like the Fragile Bond families, which appeared to live so effectively with traditional roles, these Perfect Model marriages epitomized the contemporary ideal.

Career success, healthy children, and relatively egalitarian marriages identified these couples as shining examples of modern marriage. Their divorces shocked friends, who had hoped that even though families around them were breaking apart, these couples were indeed "making it."

The three families in the last group were very different from families in all other patterns. Not only were they much younger (average age of twenty-six and twenty-four for husbands and wives), they appeared to scarcely fit the image of "family." Unlike the Perfect Model families, who presented such a secure image, these very young couples never really formed a family unit. Pregnant and married at an early age, the women rebelled against the confinement of marriage. They had difficulty forming bonds with either their husbands or babies, and they never completely accepted the role of wife or mother. Husbands were threatened by their wives' distance and refusal to accommodate to family roles. The wives' lack of concern in mothering puzzled and frightened these men. Both the short duration of these marriages and the apparent lack of bonding suggest these families were Unformed Families.

Perfect Model Marriages

David: It's obvious that many people saw ours as a model marriage, and in a superficial way it was. I realize now that it was a fantasy thing to a great extent. She really did picture me as superman and had some exaggerated views of my ability . . . In my job I have been in the position where people feel I am the problem solver . . . the one who provides support. It's a super counseling role. But you know that's a very draining kind of thing. So there were times when I had the need to cry and be free of other people's burdens, but I didn't have that in the marriage. I did resent the fact that I literally had to be the executive at home.

David had many ambivalent feelings about his marriage. He was a successful executive, and this aura of success permeated the marriage. His wife, Gail, viewed him as a very capable man and was quite possibly intimidated by his success. He fostered and commanded a "superman" image but also resented this role. As the executive in the office and at home, he was not able to reveal his weaknesses and his need for support. Perhaps he wanted Gail to sense his needs and give him permission to express the more vulnerable, unguarded sides of himself. His "superman" cloak entrapped him in emotional isolation.

These couples were in their late twenties and early thirties. Married a little over seven years, they had school-age and preschool children. Altogether these eight couples had six boys and six girls.

Three of the eight men had doctorates and were employed in universities; the other five were in business. Even though young, this group of men had achieved some status and security within their professions. Men in academia had been promoted rapidly and had excellent positions in a major university. Businessmen had positions in management or had their own businesses. Only one man was relatively insecure professionally. He had been in a number of occupations and was now employed part-time while attending school.

Two women in these families also had doctorates and were employed in a university. Two other women were highly involved in careers in education. The remaining four women quit work to be home with the children. After a couple of years at home, two of these women became restless and returned to work. The other two started working when the divorce became imminent. Regardless of the amount of time spent on the job, however, these women seemed to share a similar desire for a career and a life outside the home.

Discounting and Dismissing. In some ways, men in Perfect Model marriages resembled men in Doll's House Marriages; they appealed to their wives with persuasion and reason; they expected deference and accommodation. In subtle ways they also avoided and attacked. Their behaviors appeared to be much more flexible than other men's. They did not become locked into rigid, stereotyped responses. Perhaps their education and management positions equipped them with more diverse, sophisticated means of communication.

One repertoire of behaviors reported consistently by these families involved a series of avoidance gestures in which the man *labeled, discounted,* and *dismissed* his wife's requests. In labeling and discounting, the husband became aware of his wife's request but interpreted it as insignificant or trivial. He discounted it and then dismissed it. It was not important enough to pay attention to it. Later, he *affirmed* his actions. He had noticed the request, but he felt there was no need to respond because the wife's message lacked significance.

David, a successful business executive, maintained very long work hours and was gone from his home from early morning until late evening. His wife had three children within four years. With the unplanned pregnancy with the third child, she became depressed and began to complain to David about his absence from the family and his inattentiveness to her and the children's needs. After the divorce, David reported that immediately preceding the separation, when the third child was already four years old, he felt:

David: I really had no awareness of anything of significance until the summer before our separation . . . And then even the initial ones were rather oblique kinds of things, basically *just* arguments about my attentiveness to her and the kids [emphasis by author].

He was aware of Gail's requests, but he discounted them as "just" arguments about his attentiveness. From the time before the birth of the third child until the divorce four years later, he received these messages but discounted them as insignificant.

Sidney interpreted Barbara's postpartum depression as insignificant:

Interviewer: You mentioned something about postpartum depression. Was that pretty serious? Did it last very long?

Sidney: Evidently it was much more serious than was obvious to me, because when I saw Barbara at that time, I thought she was pretty cheerful. However, subsequently she told me she was depressed.

Interviewer: But she did not communicate that at the time?

Sidney: Well, I don't know. She might have said that she
                 felt bad, but it was not obvious to me. It was a
                 very general depression.

When Gail became more aware of her sexual needs and
demanded greater efforts toward sexual fulfillment, David discounted the significance of her needs:

David: She started to dabble in the psychological aspects of
          orgasm.

In looking back on his attitudes during marriage, David
acknowledged his "chauvinism" in dismissing female orgasms as
an expected event:

David: I was a chauvinistic or naive male, in that I accepted
          female orgasm as a part of sex but I also had sufficient
          experience to know that it didn't always happen.

Sometimes women felt their husbands were not responsive to their successful experiences outside the home. Elaine, a
college teacher, described Frank's lack of interest in her work:

Interviewer: Did he say anything about your teaching?

Elaine: No, he appeared to be completely uninterested.
                 As soon as I started to talk about it, he would
                 make some desultory conversation but then
                 would announce that it was time to go in his
                 study and play his guitar . . . I wasn't doing any-
                 thing important, so he didn't pay any atten-
                 tion.

Although labeling and discounting behavior appeared
more frequently in the husband's repertoire than in the wife's,
it was not exclusively a male pattern. Sheryl acknowledged that
she was not always attentive and responsive to her husband,
Marc:

Sheryl: We could never talk about personal things at all
                 or what we were feeling. When I tried, he wasn't
                 good at being sympathetic, or he did it in a way
                 that was not helpful . . .
Interviewer: Did he ever make any effort to try to share his
                 experiences with you?
Sheryl: He did, and I think I probably tended not to be
                 responsive, because I was so wrapped up in all of
                 my various miseries. I couldn't really see his as
                 serious. It always seemed to me that his situation
                 was much better than mine; why did he have a
                 right to complain? I now see that is a mispercep-
                 tion also.

The subtle language in each of these responses suggests
the person received a message from the spouse but evaluated it
as unworthy of a response. Gail was "dabbling" in an explora-
tion of her sexuality or "just" complaining again about his absence from home. Elaine's work was insignificant and uninteresting; Marc's problems were not serious and he had no right to
complain. Having discounted the importance of the message,
the husband or wife could then dismiss it.

Quite possibly, partners felt they were taken for granted
or not noticed. Their messages did not get a response, and behaviors continued as if the messages had never been sent.
Husbands who discounted and dismissed their wives' requests had a double advantage: they could affirm they had
heard the message and had considered it, but since it was not
important, they did not need to act on it. They could retain an
image of themselves as considerate, attentive spouses, but
they were also spared the necessity of changing objectionable
behaviors.

Layered Criticisms. Men in Perfect Model marriages were
also quite critical of their wives. Some criticisms were simply
expressed as disappointments over performance: the wife was
not a good housekeeper or was not efficient in managing the
household budget. These simple, straightforward criticisms
probably had a minor impact on the woman's self-esteem, par-

ticularly if they were directed at performance in areas of life less important to her self-identity.

Other criticisms had more impact because they continued over a period of time and involved performance in areas more central to the woman's identity. Sheryl felt vulnerable to her husband's criticisms of her as a mother:

Interviewer: While you were married, did you have any differences in your attitudes on child rearing?

Sheryl: Yes. I felt that there should be limitations. There should be some sort of discipline. I felt that as soon as a child was able to perform certain duties, such as make his bed, clean up his room, he should do so. Marc would be very impatient with that.

Interviewer: Did you try to set up some kinds of limitations? What was his attitude toward you then?

Sheryl: I tried to. Marc would either view it patronizingly as "This is some silly way to try to raise a child," or sometimes he would really be annoyed and feel like I was squashing Jeffrey . . . He made it clear that I was doing it the wrong way, and I felt I was very much under his influence psychologically, that I *was* doing it the wrong way . . . His way of doing anything was superior [emphasis by respondent] .

The most potent criticisms were *layered.* In one type of layered criticism, the husband criticized his wife for not disciplining correctly or for not providing adequate physical care of the children. However, he made a deeper judgment implying a more serious incapacity: the failure to be a "natural mother." This judgment was often not articulated but was conveyed by a hostile, accusing look or a harsh tone of voice. In subtle ways he let his wife know he did not trust her ability to be a mother:

Jason: I think she would have been inclined to be more strict than I permitted her to be. I was brought

	up without much discipline, so I tended to repeat it.
Interviewer:	Did you have disagreements on handling your children?
Jason:	Yes, especially towards the end of the marriage. We had a lot of them. And at first they were not so much disagreements as my telling her not to do it certain ways. I think I would sort of bull my way through. I think to the extent that she was trying to do something she didn't believe in, it could have been a significant contributor to her problems . . . I would often not like the way she was handling things, and I would tell her that, and it would be kind of a putdown.
Interviewer:	Did you think she was too strict or strict in a way that was not productive?
Jason:	I thought that there was an awful lot of—I seemed to detect a sense of real dislike. I felt when she was being strict, she really didn't like that kid at all. That she didn't like him or want him around. I may be dead wrong, but it really made me very uneasy.

Jeff was critical of his wife's care of the child both during the marriage and after it ended. After the divorce, he and his second wife instigated a series of meetings and an exchange of notes that conveyed their criticisms to Katrina:

Jeff:	A lot of times Billy comes over here with a cold because I don't think she's been aware of how he's dressed. She doesn't change the sheets on his bed enough when he wets the bed. I have a lot of —I don't feel he gets enough food, and he gets ignored at dinnertime, has to wait till eight or nine o'clock, doesn't get a regular schedule.
Interviewer:	Is it because she's working, perhaps, or busy?
Jeff:	Working and busy, and just tends to kind of space through it if she's having people over. I

	don't think there's a special effort to feed him. I think it's basic nurturing.
Interviewer:	It sounds, too, from what you're saying that she's very much involved in starting another life for herself, and it may be hard for her to keep as much attention on him as would be good.
Jeff:	That's one of the problems we had. She wants very much to be independent, and she also identifies with being a mother. She would really go out and fight full force for custody because she somehow would feel it would take a vital part of her.
Interviewer:	So you feel it is important to her identity as a person to think of herself as a mother?
Jeff:	Yes, and I really don't think that she—some people are just natural mothers, and honestly, I don't feel she's a natural mother . . . It's very important for her to feel that she's an adequate mother. And she gets from me that I don't feel she is. Which isn't a good situation, because I make it pretty clear.

These layered criticisms were painful for the women. They had a powerful effect because they were constant and involved issues central to the woman's identity. Furthermore, they were not refutable. Even if Katrina improved her physical care of Billy, how could she prove she was a "natural mother"? This condition is so vague it can never be documented. Accusations of inadequacy in mothering kept women anxious and willing to conform to the husband's philosophies of child rearing, even when they ran counter to their own.

A second type of layered criticism occurred when the husband was frustrated in one area of life and displaced that frustration onto his wife. Fear of failing at work aroused anxieties, which were easily discharged by angry criticisms of the wife. Jeff felt guilty about an extramarital relationship and criticized Katrina:

Jeff:	I became involved with this other woman, and I felt very guilty at the time. I took it all very seriously, and I became very emotional about it. And, really, at that point I tried to make our relationship worse. I tried to rationalize my own behavior.
Interviewer:	Tried to make it worse? How did you do that?
Jeff:	Just by being very critical of her, trying to convince myself how I really didn't care for her. I just looked at all the negative aspects of it. Just, uh, thinking of instances that showed she really didn't love me. And, uh, feeling sorry for myself, that I wasn't getting a model of perfection and what I thought I deserved as a person.

Such criticisms allowed the husband to avoid the real issues and place responsibility on his wife. These criticisms were equally difficult to combat. Even if Katrina tried to modify her behavior to meet her husband's expectations, the criticisms continued, since the couple never dealt with the real problem. In fact, if Katrina made positive changes, the focus would shift to another area of life, and the criticisms could become even more intense.

The Model Marriage: Burdens and Ambiguities. These behaviors of demanding, discounting, and criticizing conveyed a powerful message to women. The wife's profession and personal needs were secondary to her husband's; her performance was somewhat inferior and left something to be desired. The implication was that a model of perfection existed, a model of the natural mother, the loving wife. She never quite made it to that level of perfection and, hence, was never quite acceptable:

Sheryl:	He had all these levels I had to reach before he would accept me completely. When I got to these levels, he changed them and wanted something else . . . I was constantly never quite making it all the way . . . He never gave me credit for trying . . . He always had a reason for backing away from me.

Sheryl believed that at the times when they were the closest, he backed away:

Sheryl: To him when things were going their best, he was the
             most worried. And he would change it so we weren't
             getting along. He could create another problem that
             would push me away. He was always pushing me
             away.

The Perfect Model served as an excellent device for distancing in marriage. Since the wife could never attain the expected levels, the man could rationalize his minimal commitment to the marriage. He could give himself more freely to his career and interests outside the relationship. Moreover, he could maintain an image of himself as superior—superior in his parenting ability, in his professional performance, and in his sexual desirability. The projection of these expectations gave him control within the relationship. Jason described his wife's reaction to his extramarital relationship early in the marriage:

Jason: She understood me very well. Sometimes when I
                  would do strange things, she would make allow-
                  ances for that . . . She was a very understanding
                  person.
Interviewer: I suppose she must have gotten upset about it
                  during the early part of your marriage.
Jason: She did. I always had a lot of control over her.
                  Even though she was upset, I was somehow able
                  to smooth it over.
Interviewer: How did you smooth it over?
Jason: Mostly through being affectionate, and sitting
                  down and talking with her and stuff like that.

This type of control could continue, however, only as long as the wife agreed with her husband's definition of their relative status. As long as she was willing to meet his standards of housekeeping and accept his methods of child rearing, she acknowledged him as superior in the home. As she arranged her own life and schedule to give his career priority, she demonstrated that his professional life was more important. If she felt she wasn't getting enough support from the relationship and blamed herself for needing too much, she conveyed the message that his minimal commitment was acceptable. As she allowed him to escape emotionally from the marriage, she implied her needs were not significant.

This dependency created problems for both the husband and wife. The woman's need for support began to be burdensome for him. Don resented Sharon's dependency and felt he was being drained:

Don: She needed comfort; there's nothing wrong with that. Maybe I was lax in providing some of the support sometimes to her emotionally. Because, you know, somehow I felt she was tapping a reservoir that was going to be emptied pretty quick. And I couldn't do it all the time. I refused to do it. I felt like I was doing enough.

David felt he could never depend on Gail for sustenance and support. As indicated earlier, he resented his "superman" role:

David: She really did picture me as superman and had some exaggerated views of my ability. After six or seven years of reality, she saw that I had some frailties; that was very difficult for her to cope with . . . I did resent the fact that I literally had to be the executive at home.

Like other men in these marriages, David found it difficult to communicate a message of personal need:

Interviewer: Did you ever tell her some of the things that were bothering you about your work and try to get support from her?

David: In fairness to her, she would say no. From my point of view, I thought I was. The only thing,

when we talk about that, there is extreme pressure on the job, the last thing I wanted to do was
go home and talk about it. It would be very difficult for me . . .

Interviewer: What did you want from her at those times? If
problems at work were distressing you and you'd
go home feeling really drained, what would you
have liked?

David: Just an understanding of that.

Many ambiguities were present in these marriages. The
husband cast himself in the role of a competent, successful professional. He assumed his marriage would fit in around his career. He fantasized a perfect model of marriage that placed a
great deal of pressure on him and his wife. He expected her to
aspire to this ideal model and criticized her when she fell short.
His intelligence, success, and high expectations quite possibly
intimidated his wife. She played the game by his rules and struggled to meet his expectations. As she did so, she became increasingly dependent on him, as her performance was always judged
by his standards. Eventually her dependency became burdensome and he felt trapped by the super-role. Easing out of this
role was not easy, for he did not know how to express his vulnerability or behave in a way that would elicit the comfort and
support he craved. His super-role isolated him.

However, changing this role was also threatening. When
women began achieving success in their own professions and became less dependent, tensions within the marriage increased. Although these men said they wanted their wives to be independent, they were confused and threatened by movements toward
independence. Sheryl recalled:

Sheryl: It was understood, and for a couple of years it was
the case, that he was the one whose interests had to
be satisfied. So the idea was that it was all right for me
to work as long as I was not in direct competition
with him. As soon as there was any possibility that
my doing something might detract from his career, I

think he got very nervous. . . . I was coming into my own, and I think that scared him very much.

Elaine told a similar story:

Elaine: When I look back and try to see when it was that he started to run around with other women, I think it was right after I got the job at the university. Prior to that point I think he was always able to feel superior to me. When he was an undergraduate, I was employed as a social worker, and that was not a particularly high-status occupation. Then he was a graduate student and all I had was a B.A. I went back to graduate school.

Interviewer: Did he finish before you did?

Elaine: Yes. Then all of a sudden we both had jobs. I didn't have a social worker or a graduate-type job. I had a faculty position. On top of that I was getting very involved in campus matters and doing all sorts of things. I would come home and be very happy and he would be sitting playing his guitar. He played the guitar four hours a night. I think what happened is that he finally had to acknowledge that I was competitive.

Job status and increased self-confidence translated into more power within the home. Jason said that his marriage broke up when Jeanne went back to work after being at home for several years.

Interviewer: How did you feel about her work?

Jason: That's the thing that broke up the marriage. All of a sudden she got this real independent attitude. Finally she was making some money on her own, and there was a *definite* change as soon as she started working [emphasis by respondent].

Husbands were ambivalent about their wives' changes.

Marc's eventual rejection of Sheryl's increased independence confused her:

Sheryl: He said, "I have to leave, you are too dependent." He felt very confused and upset, and I would have done anything to preserve the marriage. So he would keep telling me things that I should do that would make me more independent and he would love me more. Each time I did one of these independent things, I discovered that it was perfectly all right, and I was able to do even more. And each time he would draw away from me a little more, so that the more I did what he seemed to want me to do and become independent— and, of course, this is one of our double-bind paradoxes, you become independent by getting directions from him on how to do it—but, nevertheless, the more I did these things that he seemed to want me to do, the more he would withdraw. I think that he really believed that he would like it better if I could lead an independent life, but each time I did, his level of anxiety would rise, so that he had to get away from me.

As women began to draw support from alternative sources outside the marriage, including their own careers and friendships, their need to accept the husband's standards changed. They set their own standards for performance both within the home as parents and homemakers and on the job. The image of a Perfect Model failed; with the failure of that image, the husband's control diminished. Jason moved out when he found out he no longer could control his wife. His wife, Jeanne, had become involved in an extramarital relationship. Although he himself had been involved in a number of relationships throughout the marriage, he had not expected this behavior from her.

Jason: I got very angry. At the same time I realized all that stuff that she had been through when I was doing all that; in fact, I remember having told her before that if she ever did anything like that, I was going to leave. All of a sudden, then, she did that. And yet, I didn't want to leave. I wanted to preserve the marriage. I was kind of put out for a while. After about two weeks and it wasn't getting any better, it was getting worse, I realized I had no control anymore. I had no affection from her.

In one of these eight marriages, the wife, Barbara, initiated the divorce. In the other seven, the husbands moved out when they became uncomfortable with the changes in their wives' attitudes and behaviors. One contributing factor to divorce in each of these marriages was conflict over the wife's dependent/independent role. Although the men seemed to favor more independence in their wives, they had a great deal of difficulty coping with that actual behavior.

Both the men and women in these marriages experienced some sorrow and sadness when their marriages ended, but they coped very well with the divorce. They were unusually competent, rational people. They appeared to know how to locate the resources they needed for their own recovery. They sought counseling if they felt they needed it; they experimented with new ways to meet people and begin dating relationships. They were very much involved in their careers, and they moved through the weeks and months following the divorce with a kind of certainty and confidence not often found in the men and women in the other patterns.

In five of the eight families, the father gained custody. The unique characteristic of these families, however, was their approach to custody; of all the families in this study, these families achieved more of a shared arrangement with the children after the divorce. It was clearly less important whether the mother or father had legal or physical custody. Both parents remained very much involved. Both mothers and fathers were nurturing and effective parents during the marriage; this continued after the divorce.

Unformed Families

Interviewer: What was the chief problem in your marriage?
Bonnie: Well, I can't really answer that because I don't know. I have no idea. The way I put it, I went

> crazy. I don't know why I left with Jack . . . My
> lawyer said that I was very immature. That's all
> I kept on hearing, was that I was very immature.
> He said I didn't know what I wanted and that I
> was all mixed up. I should go see a psychiatrist
> because I didn't know what I wanted.

Bonnie was confused about her marriage and divorce. In looking back on her short marriage, she felt it might have been a mistake from the very beginning. Married at the age of nineteen, she had an unplanned child within a year. Within two years after that, she had a second child, also unplanned. Left at home with two infants, she felt trapped and desperate. Perhaps her affair with Jack was the means for abandoning her overwhelming responsibilities. She left quite abruptly but returned after two months. During that period of time, she decided that although she did not wish to stay married to Joel, she did want to live with her children.

Lack of Bonding. These three families shared several characteristics that made them strikingly different from other families. They were young when they married. Two women were eighteen and nineteen; the third was in her mid-twenties. Bonnie had two unplanned children. Karen reluctantly had a child after her husband convinced her it would be desirable. Debra wanted a child and convinced her husband, Ron, that it was time to have one. Ron was reluctant because their marriage was not strong. He consented, hoping the baby would make his wife happier.

Children had a stressful impact on all three young couples. The women were tense and nervous about caring for infants and resented being home alone all day. They missed the stimulation of school and work. Their husbands tried to help and often got up at night with the baby. They were concerned about their wives' difficulties in coping with the infant. Bruce worried about Karen's apparent lack of love for their child:

Bruce: She took excellent care of the baby, but I guess it was
           from her family background. She lacked the love to

give the baby. She really didn't have the mother instinct. He was always fed well, bathed, had clean clothes, everything essential except for love.

Like the other husbands, Bruce interpreted his wife's restlessness and anxiety as a rejection of the child. He believed many of her attitudes with the child originated in her own unstable and troubled childhood.

A second problem arose as these women, nervous with the care of an infant, sought help from their mothers. Bruce described this as one of the primary problems within the marriage.

Bruce: It's not so much that her mother interfered, but my ex-wife always asked *her* for advice. She wouldn't think anything out for herself; she wouldn't ask me for any kind of advice.

Distancing from the husbands also increased as the women became less responsive sexually. Bonnie recalled a change in attitude toward sex after the arrival of the first child:

Interviewer: Did the baby have any effect upon your sex life?

Bonnie: That was sort of disrupted. I didn't want to have sex after I had my child. Just never. I was too nervous.

Interviewer: Were you afraid of having another child?

Bonnie: No. No, I just really, I felt there was no need to have sex.

Interviewer: I suppose your husband must have been pretty disappointed. Did he get angry?

Bonnie: No. I never said no. We more or less had sex but without me getting into it. I did not want to have sex.

Men complained about their wives' coldness; they felt they were not physically responsive, did not like to touch, and shared little intimacy. They tended to attribute this coldness to earlier family life and unfavorable childhood experiences. They realized their wives were much less committed to both the marriage and parenting than they were.

These three marriages all shared the same characteristic: the woman's lack of bonding with the child and husband. Young when married, these women had children before experiencing intimacy within the marriage. Still tied to their mothers, they went to them for help rather than to their husbands. Viewed within the marital context, their behaviors appeared immature. However, in another context these behaviors might have been judged differently. For example, nineteen-year-old unmarried female college students who show a continuing attachment to their mothers and occasionally return to them for help with problems are not generally viewed as immature. Similarly, young adults normally explore different social relationships. These behaviors, which may be considered developmentally appropriate for persons in their late teens and early twenties, appeared immature and selfish within the context of marriage and parenting.

Lack of Self-Awareness. A second characteristic shared by these young women was a lack of awareness and understanding of their own behaviors. They were very confused and could not explain why they had left their husbands and babies. As Bonnie put it, she felt she "went crazy."

Other people did not assist them in understanding their behavior. As they proceeded through the divorce, they encountered physicians, lawyers, relatives, and friends who labeled them "immature." Bonnie reported her lawyer felt she was too immature to raise children and should see a psychiatrist. Husbands and in-laws were particularly harsh in judging these young women.

Bonnie and Karen eventually left their husbands and babies. Bonnie returned after two months and resumed care of her children, but Karen did not return. In the third family, Debra asked Ron to leave; she kept the child with her. All three husbands were quite disappointed with the brevity of their marriage and confused about the reasons for its failure.

6

Children's Roles
in Family Politics

Like actors in a play on stage, children assume a part in the family drama. The roles they are assigned to play are shaped by parents' demands and expectations. Men and women who have made parenting the focal point of their lives may encourage children to be dependent and "connected" to them; conversely, men and women who resent parenting and find it burdensome may try to limit their children's intrusion upon their lives. Parents who are losing a power struggle within the family or on the job and who become victims or martyrs may need children who respond solicitously with concern and even guilt.

As parents approach a divorce, a child may assume one of five roles: Stabilizer, Competitor, Hostage, Obstacle, or Caretaker. These roles are not simply temporary, short-term reactions to divorce. They are rooted in past family history and were molded slowly over a period of time by the actions of all participants. How do these roles form? How, for example, does power, as it is played out by the husband and wife, shape and create a Caretaking role for the child? How do coercive power and prolonged stress contribute to the development of the Hostage role for children? Why and how do coalitions form within the family? What impact do they have on the marital and parenting relationship?

In two important ways, this chapter will differ from previous chapters. Instead of focusing exclusively on husband/wife relationships, I will discuss the children's roles in the family. I will show how they are affected by the marriage and how, in turn, they influence the husband/wife relationship. Second, instead of tracing the paths from initial family formation to separation and divorce, I will start by examining the end point—family life during the period of separation and divorce. Then I will look at past events that shaped the present family life. Thus, I will be viewing divorce and custody from a second perspective to point up the complexity of family life.

When a family separates, two dimensions within the parent/child relationship become important. First, the family must address the issue of physical division: Which parent will be responsible for the daily physical support and management of the children? This parent, through physical proximity and availability, will have greater opportunity to interact with the children and retain an important place in their lives.

The second dimension may, however, be even more important than physical division of the family. The quality of each parent's relationship with the children may affect their development more than physical arrangements of custody. Warmth, affection, and effective discipline are critical to the child's physical, mental, and emotional well-being. Parents in this study varied greatly on this dimension. In the interviews some men and women revealed a high degree of both nurturance and efficacy as they talked about their children. They revealed warm, accepting attitudes and an active, intelligent involvement in parenting. They felt responsible for guiding their children—what they did made a difference. They were confident that their disciplinary methods were effective and appropriate.

On the other end of the continuum were parents who appeared to be much less involved with their children. They voiced relatively little concern for their problems. They did not appear to enjoy or seek out their children's company and spent little time with them. Often these men and women were less sure of themselves as parents; they lacked confidence in disciplining their children. They were either not consistent or not sure that what they were doing was effective.

Parents ranged from those who appeared highly nurturing and effective to those who appeared low in both these qualities. Many parents, of course, were not on either extreme but clustered toward the center of the continuum. And there were a few parents who appeared good at one thing but not another. For example, some parents appeared warm, nurturing, and loving but unskillful in guiding and disciplining their children. They were concerned with their lack of efficacy with the children. Other parents appeared to be more sure of themselves and capable of guiding and disciplining their children but expressed little warmth and affection toward them. In a few cases parents revealed rather cold and even hostile attitudes toward their children.

In this chapter I will use these two important dimensions of physical custody and parental effectiveness as a basis for defining and describing five different parenting arrangements. I used a circle diagram (Figure 1) to represent these five patterns because a circle suggests continuity; there are no end points. When considering family behaviors, I believe it is more useful to think in terms of a continuum or range of behaviors; a circle best projects this image of continuity and overlapping.

Figure 1 indicates a circle with the two dimensions as intersecting axes. The horizontal axis is physical custody; families located above the horizontal line are mother-custody families, and families below it are father-custody families. The vertical axis depicts parental effectiveness. In the right portion of the circle are families in which both parents appeared to be highly nurturing, effective, and capable. Located to the left of the vertical line are those families with lower levels of nurturance and efficacy. Clustered around the vertical axis are those

Figure 1. Parent/Child Bonds and Physical Custody
in Five Parenting Patterns.

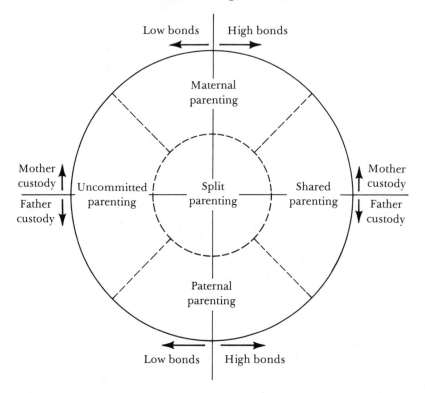

families in which one parent was clearly effective, warm, and responsible and the second parent was less effective.

Using the two axes, the circle may be divided into five
areas, with the families in each area representing a particular
type of parenting arrangement. For convenience and economy,
I will refer to five groups although in reality these families are
more accurately viewed as located on a continuum around the
circle. Thirty-eight of the forty families are located in this circle. Two families are not included in analysis since their hus-
band/wife, parent/child patterns were quite different, and they
could not be located within this analytic framework.

On the far right of the circle are the Shared Parenting
families. Before the divorce both parents within these families

demonstrated high levels of nurturance and potency with their children (Table 6). In seven of these eight families, the mother

Table 6. Nurturance and Efficacy in Five Parenting Patterns.

Parenting Pattern	Nurturance[a]		Efficacy	
	Women	Men	Women	Men
Shared (8)	4.0	4.3	3.9	4.4
Maternal (6)	4.2	2.7	3.8	3.2
Uncommitted (8)	2.8	2.9	2.9	3.1
Paternal (10)	3.0	4.4	2.6	3.9
Split				
(Doll's House 3)	4.6	3.3	4.0	3.0
(Fractured 3)	5.0	3.3	2.3	3.7
Group mean	3.6	3.6	3.3	3.7

[a]Interview segments were used to assess each respondent on nurturance and efficacy. Scales extended from 1 to 5, with higher numbers representing higher nurturance or efficacy. Numbers in this table represent mean scores achieved by respondents in each group.

received custody, but both parents remained highly involved with their children after the separation. The children assumed a role of *Stabilizer* to both parents, a role described more fully later in this chapter. In husband/wife interaction, most of these eight families were characterized as Perfect Model families (Table 7). Thus, these couples tended to be younger, better educated, and more sophisticated in their attempts to control the marital relationship.

Maternal Parenting families are located around the top of the circle. Most of these couples, as Fragile Bond families, followed traditional roles during their marriage. These mothers assumed a more primary role in parenting and appeared to be more nurturing and effective (Table 6). All six women in this group received custody of their children. Fathers were less involved and assumed less responsibility for everyday matters of discipline and management. For some fathers, the child became a *Competitor* for the woman's love and attention; for the women, however, the children assumed the role of *Stabilizer*.

Clustered around the horizontal axis on the far left are the Uncommitted Parenting families. These Uncommitted Par-

Table 7. Parenting and Marital Patterns.

Parenting Pattern	Physical Custody[a]	Child's Role[b]		Predominant Marital Pattern[c]
Shared	Mother (7)	Stabilizer	(M)	Perfect Model
	Father (1)	Stabilizer	(F)	
Maternal	Mother (6)	Stabilizer	(M)	Fragile Bond
	Father (0)	Competitor	(F)	
Uncommitted	Mother (4)	Hostage	(M)	Fractured Families
	Father (4)	Hostage	(F)	Unformed Families
Paternal	Mother (0)	Obstacle	(M)	Stalemate
	Father (10)	Stabilizer	(F)	Mixture of families from other patterns
Split	Mother (2)	Caretaker or		Fractured Families
	Father (4)	Stabilizer	(M & F)	Doll's House

[a]Numbers in this column indicate the number of families with mother or father custody.

[b]In this column *M* designates Mother, or the role the child played for the mother. *F* designates Father, or the child/father role.

[c]With the exception of Paternal Parenting, in which marital patterns were mixed, parenting groups were composed mainly of families from one or two marital patterns. Correlations of marital and parenting patterns, however, were not perfect. Thus, in the Shared Parenting group, six families were Perfect Model and two were from other patterns. In Maternal Parenting, five were Fragile Bond Families and one was from another pattern. The marital pattern listed designates the predominant pattern(s) in each group.

enting families included four mother- and four father-custody families. In comparison with other parents, these men and women were less nurturing and effective (Table 6). They revealed a minimal emotional commitment to their parenting role and a low level of potency. Most of these eight families were characterized as either Fractured or Unformed Families; their children served as *Hostages* or pawns in the continuing marital warfare (Table 7).

On the lower part of the circle are *Paternal Parenting* families. In these father-custody families, the father became the more dominant parent. At the time of divorce, he appeared to be more nurturing and effective in his relationship with the children (Table 6). These families are similar to Maternal Parenting families in that one parent became increasingly more dominant in the parenting role as the family lived together. Children played a *Stabilizer* role for the father but were *Obstacles* for women, who felt frustrated and resentful with parenting responsibilities. The ten families in this group represented a variety of marital patterns.

In the center of the circle are the *Split Parenting* families. In some of these families, one parent was more nurturing but the second was more effective in managing the children; in other families, the child identified with and chose one parent even though the other parent appeared more nurturing and effective. These families are split because each parent served a different function for the child and the child was often split in his or her loyalties to both parents. Children usually assumed a *Caretaker* role with one parent and a *Stabilizer* role with the other parent. These families, who included three Fractured Families and three Doll's House Marriages, had quite complicated family interaction patterns. They had difficulty resolving physical custody. In four families the father had custody, and in two, the mother (Table 7).

In summary, children played roles as Stabilizers, Competitors, Hostages, Obstacles, and Caretakers in these five parenting patterns. The five parenting patterns—Maternal, Shared, Uncommitted, Paternal, and Split—were shaped by the husbands' and wives' interaction patterns.

The Child as Stabilizer: Shared Parenting

Remarkable among these eight families was the high degree of cooperation achieved in child rearing after the divorce. In these families, both parents appeared to be nurturing, capable parents; they continued to be very involved with their children after the divorce.

Most of these families were in the Perfect Model pattern, and they shared similarities in their histories. First, the status of the men and women in these marriages was more equal than in other family types. These women retained a higher level of self-esteem because they had greater access to support from outside the family and experienced a minimum of coercive power within the marriage. They were successful in their work and received a great deal of satisfaction from this. They were financially more independent and could survive without the husband's income. They identified less with their husbands; during the course of their marriage, they were able to move from an idealization of their mate into a more healthy and realistic assessment. Continued contact with people outside the marriage through work and friendships undoubtedly helped them attain a more realistic image of themselves, their mates, and their marriages.

Men in the Shared Parenting families were successful in retaining their high status within the marriage. Subtle avoidance and attack behaviors sustained some emotional distance within the relationship and enabled them to retain control, but these powering behaviors were not debilitating to the woman's esteem. Powering behaviors used by both men and women remained relatively subtle and never escalated into a destructive, coercive level.

Stress in childbearing and child rearing was minimal (Table 8). These couples had small families, with an average of only

Table 8. Stress in Parenting Among Families in Five Parenting Patterns.

Parenting Pattern	Percentage of Unplanned Children	Number of Children	Stress During Pregnancy/Infancy Period, 1st Child	Conflict in Child Rearing
Shared	27	1.4	Low to moderate	Low
Maternal	50	2.3	Low to moderate	Moderate
Uncommitted	64	2.9	High	High
Paternal	25	2.0	High for women Low for men	High
Split	27	1.8	Low to moderate	Moderate

1.4 children per family. Some men and women experienced stress during the pregnancy with the first child, particularly when these children were not planned. However, after the birth of the child, stress was reduced, and the couple encountered very few serious problems with child rearing. In some families, women were uncomfortable with their husband's critical attitudes about child rearing, but generally the parents were able to work together and share parenting responsibilities.

For most of these parents, children were *Stabilizers.* They provided meaning and an opportunity to create structure in life. The child's presence encouraged adults to place energy into creating a home and family life. The everyday tasks of maintaining a house and a job were more meaningful in the context of family life. Children also provided parents with an avenue for expressing love and affection. Men and women received satisfaction from their relationship with their children. Although they recognized that the presence of children demanded certain sacrifices, they evaluated the positive aspects of parenting as outweighing increased demands and responsibilities.

Physical custody was not an issue for these parents. Men who did not have custody felt assured that at some future time their children might elect to live with them. They appeared to experience little loss or fear that their children would grow away from them, a fear expressed more frequently by men in the Maternal Parenting families. These men felt assured and confident that they would retain an important role in their children's lives. Some looked forward to assuming full responsibilities in the future but indicated that at present they could not handle full custodial responsibilities. They wanted time to devote to their careers and to school; they were also becoming involved with new partners. Thus, a shared arrangement was preferable to full legal and physical custody.

The children in these families probably were least affected by the divorce. They were assured of both parents' continuing interest. Their loyalties were not torn between their parents, and they were not used as hostages between two embittered and angry adults.

Living arrangements were remarkably fluid. In three homes, the parents had experimented with different arrangements. One couple started with a joint arrangement in which the child spent half the week in each home. When the mother moved and got a new and more demanding job, the arrangement shifted, the father caring for the child during the week and the mother assuming responsibilities on weekends. In another family, the mother retained responsibility for the two small children immediately after the divorce. When the father became settled in a new residence, the children spent more time with him and divided their time between the two parents. For a third family, the child remained with his father during the separation period. The couple reasoned that since the mother was involved in a new relationship, the child's needs would be better served by remaining in his own home with his father. Later, when the woman's relationship dissolved and the father became very busy with school and work, the mother assumed more responsibility for the child. These families were able to remain fluid and change periodically as the needs of the children and parents changed.

(The only difficulties arose when children became confused about the arrangements. When that happened, one parent generally gave up some time in order to give the children a primary home location. There were no reports by parents of major disturbances among the children, of guilt or anger, as so frequently reported by other families.

The age of the children was possibly important; none of these children had reached the teen years. Since most of them were still preschoolers, it may have been easier for these families to achieve a degree of flexibility. For children of this young age, maintaining time with both parents was more important than spending time with neighborhood peer groups. They had not developed the complicated schedules and peer-group associations so characteristic of older children.

Perhaps the men's and women's young age and relatively brief marriages also helped them achieve a shared role. They had not accumulated a great deal of bitterness toward each other. They were still young, attractive, and able to find mates. They had plentiful resources in their occupations, money, and friends in the community and were able to use these resources in creating new lives for themselves.

The Child as Competitor: Maternal Parenting

Within the Maternal Parenting group, mothers were considerably higher than fathers in both efficacy and nurturance

(Table 6). These mothers were quite clearly more dominant parents before the divorce, and they retained custody after the divorce. Like families in the Shared Parenting group, children assumed the role of *Stabilizers* for these women (Table 7).

Fathers varied in their involvement from those who had a strong commitment to the parenting role to those who had little commitment to or interest in this role. Fathers with more commitment were similar to men in the Shared Parenting group. Fathers who were less involved tended to perceive the children as *Competitors* in their relationship with their wives. Some of these men believed the child's arrival changed the tenor of the couple's bond. In more severe cases, husbands equated the child's birth with the death of the marriage. In other families these feelings were less intense, and men simply recognized that the child's demands reduced the amount of time the couple had for each other.

The families in this group shared a common type of process within the marriage. Five of the six families in this group were Fragile Bond families (Table 7). Following their traditional roles of homemaking and working, husbands and wives separated themselves from each other. They had difficulty creating a shared reality because they could not communicate or express their emotions. They were more likely than families in other patterns to retain separate definitions of their marriage and family life.

These families experienced relatively little stress with family planning and childbearing (Table 8). The conception of the first child was generally greeted with pleasure and happiness, even if the child was not planned. Perhaps these men's and women's values contributed to their defining this event as positive. They believed one of the purposes in marriage was to rear children; children represented fulfillment of marriage.

Both men and women reported a moderate amount of conflict in child rearing, more than the Shared Parenting families. This conflict was most often related to the place the children occupied in relation to the marriage. The degree to which each parent was involved with the children and the relative priority of parental and marital demands were issues within these families.

Because of the separation of roles within the marriage and the woman's assumption of responsibility for the children, the mother and children tended to form an *inclusive coalition*; the father was invited to participate, but he seldom did. Many activities took place in his absence, and the children, from birth, were associated primarily with the mother.

The women's status within the marriage and their access to work and social opportunities outside the marriage were also associated with their parenting behavior. One of the more interesting aspects of the women's relationship to the outside world was the way in which these women approached these alternative resources. Most of them were not employed, and even if they were, their job was definitely secondary to the parenting/mothering role. This did not change during the marriage. Thus, the woman's access to work and her use of work were not a threat to the husband. Women had friends, but again, these were not a threat to the marital life. Friendships were generally formed with other women with similar values; time and energy spent in cultivating friendships and a social life outside the home seldom interfered with the home role. These women generally did not pursue extramarital relationships with men. Although these opportunities existed for a few women, their commitment to the marriage and their strong ideological commitments to traditional female roles made it difficult for them to pursue such relationships. Thus, whatever access these individual women may have had to outside resources, they chose to protect their marriage and family life. They did not cultivate either work or social experiences that might have threatened or offered competition to family life.

Because of their role as homemakers and their restricted use of outside resources, these women did suffer a lower status within the marriage. However, this lower status did not adversely affect their ability to function well in the parenting role. They saw themselves as effective, loving mothers. Their success in and satisfaction with this role made them less dependent on the husband's judgment and approval. They were also protected by the separation of roles. They were less vulnerable to the husband's influence because they retained a definition of themselves and of the marriage separate from their husbands. Thus, although the status of these women did drop in their marriage, they were in less jeopardy than women in other families.

The sex and age of the children in these families had little impact on the family's decisions on custody or parenting patterns. Both male and female children, regardless of age, remained with the mother and did not consider living with their father. Even families with adolescent boys and girls did not consider splitting the family, with the females living with the mother and the males with the father.

The Child as Hostage: Uncommitted Parenting

Parents in the third group, Uncommitted Parenting, all shared a similar loss of bonding with their children. Women in this group appeared less nurturing and accepting of their children than women in other groups. They expressed less confidence in their ability to discipline and guide their children; compared with women in the Maternal Parenting group, for example, they were less sure about themselves as parents, and they assumed less responsibility for their children. Men were moderately effective with their children but did not express a great deal of warmth or involvement with their children.

The important feature of this group of families is that *both* parents were less involved with their children. In the other parenting groups, at least one parent was able to retain an effective relationship with the children, but in this group both men and women had difficulty with parenting at every period in the family cycle (Table 8). By the time of the divorce, both parents were attempting to escape their parental commitments. They made little effort to protect the child from their own anger or the rejection of the other parent. These children were more exposed to rejection than children in other groups. In the worst of conditions, children served as *Hostages* or pawns as they were used by each parent to retaliate against the mate.

In half the families, the first child was not planned, and both parents were emotionally distressed with the news of the conception. In seven of the eight families, the first child was conceived either before the marriage or during the first year of marriage. The premature conception contributed to two marital problems. First, it forced the couple to redefine their relationship. Some couples were in early stages of their relationship and had not thought of their relationship as permanent. Conception of a child created a crisis; they felt forced into a commitment to a permanent relationship before they were emotionally ready for this commitment. For a variety of social, emotional, and moral reasons, they did not choose an abortion. Second, they had less time to develop bonds with each other. Even if they were married and committed to a permanent relationship, they needed time to develop these marital bonds. Conception of a child forced them to reorder priorities. They had to rearrange work and school schedules; the male particularly felt compelled to work harder.

Thus, the pregnancy period was a time of reorganization. Emotional problems that emerged during this period included depression, anxiety, and anger. For some couples, support systems were jeopardized, as friends and kin expressed disapproval of a forced marriage. A multitude of financial, social, and emotional problems emerged during this period, along with a reduction in support from other persons, in particular, in-laws. Thus, these couples had little opportunity to positively prepare for and anticipate the child's arrival.

The period following the birth of the child was accompanied by relatively high stress for the women and moderate stress for the men. For some of the very young women, the child's demands and needs interfered with their own development. Isolation within the home frustrated their needs for social stimulation; lack of connection with people and events outside the home inhibited intellectual development. They felt a premature closure on the development of their own identity. They also felt a loss of control and lack of power, as they perceived limited alternatives to their situation. This sense of powerlessness was increased by a sense of overwhelming responsibility for the infant's well-being and fear of their own inadequacy in providing this care.

Fathers experienced this period as somewhat less stressful, probably because their exposure to the problems of caring for the child was limited to a few hours a day and their work and social routines often continued without interruption.

Stress continued through the years as these families were not able to control the timing and spacing of their children. They continued having children and ultimately had about three (2.9) children each (Table 8); thus, these families were larger than the families in other parenting groups. This failure to plan adequately suggests marital difficulties in communication. They did not seem to be able to define together an environment that would benefit themselves and their children. Or, if they did agree on some mutual goal, they were not able to attain it. They were often in the position of coping with unplanned events; family histories were characterized by frequent, prolonged periods of stress that exhausted resources within themselves and within the marriage, leaving them feeling depleted and deprived.

With the heavy demands on their time and energy and insufficient attention given to restoring marital bonds, they experienced great conflicts in raising children. Issues of control surfaced as parents disagreed on the best ways to manage their children. Issues in nurturing arose as each parent felt overloaded and attempted to engage the other parent more actively. Resentments flared as one parent perceived the other parent's attempts to disengage from the family and escape to pursuits outside the family.

By the end of the marriage, the parents in some of these families were alternating in their escapes from the home. For a short period, a wife left home as soon as her husband returned from work. She attended classes or went out with her friends. Or the husband found ways to physically separate his family from his place of work. He moved the family residence a long distance from it, so he would have to live in a separate residence during the week and could visit the family on weekends only. These escape patterns aroused anger in the other partner, who was left with responsibility for the children. In retaliation, the burdened parent resourcefully reorganized the pattern and found new ways to disengage, leaving the other parent responsible.

In addition to stress in the parent/child relationship, several of these women suffered from their husbands' verbal and physical abuse. Four of these eight families were in a marital pattern (Fractured Families) that proved particularly debilitating for women. Men in these families threatened, physically attacked, and withheld themselves sexually and emotionally. The husbands' use of coercive power and the women's subsequent loss of self-esteem decreased the women's effectiveness with their children, particularly male children. Women who used drugs or alcohol and were dependent in work and living lost the respect of their children, particularly as they became teenagers.

Stress in the family and the family's final dissolution had a severe impact on children; these children suffered a great deal. They felt guilty if they believed they had "pushed" one parent out of the home by aligning themselves with the other parent. They felt anxious, for they could never secure approval from both parents at any one time. They feared that their alignment with one parent triggered rejection from the other. Unable to tolerate this anxiety, some children attempted to shuttle back and forth between the parents after the divorce, assuring themselves of the love of each parent. This "yo-yo" situation increased insecurity, for decisions on placement of children were often made impulsively and emotionally, with little deliberation on their interests or needs.

The child's development was further hindered by the parents' preoccupations with the marital battle and their inability to separate the child from this battle. The child's own emotional needs and fears were submerged in the parents' anger and hostility.

Children in these families who appeared to fare the worst were teenage girls who lived with their fathers. They had difficulty in their relationship with their father if they resembled their mother. The physical resemblance of the girl to the mother or her emotional identification with her mother provoked intense anger within the father; the girl then became the object of punitive treatment and abuse. Teenage boys living with their fathers fared better, since they were able to identify with the father and cooperated with him in rejecting the mother.

The Child as Obstacle: Paternal Parenting

Like women in the Uncommitted Parenting families, women in the Paternal Parenting group were less involved with and interested in the parenting role. Their husbands, however, were attentive fathers and resembled men in the Shared Parenting group in their attitudes and behaviors. In all ten families in this group, fathers retained custody of the children.

The ten families in the Paternal Parenting group included three families from the Stalemate marital pattern plus seven families from other marital patterns. This group thus included a variety of marital patterns, unlike other parenting arrangements, which were composed mainly of one or two marital patterns.

What all these families did have in common was that these women rejected the *structure* of family life; they found their roles as mothers and wives rigid, confining, and depriving. Gradually, they began to see their children as *obstacles* to the development of their own interests. In contrast, men felt the family structure was useful and functional, since the children and family unit added security and meaning to their lives. For them the children were *Stabilizers*. Thus, one of the chief problems these couples faced was a discrepancy in their perceptions of the structure and meaning of family life. These differences in perception began immediately following the birth of the first child and continued until separation and divorce; they were never resolved.

These families had relatively little trouble planning children. Most of their children (75 percent) were planned (Table 8). Compared with couples in other parenting patterns, they had very little difficulty during the pregnancy period. They anticipated their first child's birth with pleasure and experienced a minimal amount of stress in making the necessary arrangements in space and finances. Support systems remained intact, since these couples, with only a few exceptions, were married and were conforming to social expectations.

Two women had some difficulty, however, because their husbands persuaded them to become pregnant. Marc threatened

to divorce his wife if she did not cooperate. However, once
pregnant, the women were not unhappy. They felt relief in resolving this issue. Sheryl, in particular, was very frightened and
anxious about having a child. This fear diminished somewhat
during her pregnancy:

Sheryl: I have always felt a great reluctance to be a mother
           ... Marc never really saw why I felt such fright and
           great apprehension at the thought of motherhood.
           He thought I was just afraid of the responsibility, but
           I knew in my heart that there was some kind of aw-
           ful terror down there that I didn't know how to deal
           with. I couldn't make it fully conscious ... Then he
           said that either I would have a child or he would di-
           vorce me ... I was terrified at the thought of being
           alone, so I settled down to have a baby. During the
           time I was pregnant, I enjoyed the pregnancy. I guess
           I felt I was finally doing the right thing, the socially
           sanctioned thing ... Our relationship during that time
           was better because I felt I was finally being a good
           wife and he felt he was achieving his goal.

The period immediately following birth was a very stressful time for all ten women but not for the men (Table 8). Even
those women who had looked forward to having a baby were
disappointed and frustrated with the actual experience. They
felt very isolated from social contacts and bored with the lack
of intellectual stimulation. They were physically fatigued by the
demands of babies who refused to sleep or were upset and cried.

They experienced a narrowing of their own identities and
began to see themselves as uninteresting persons with a limited
range of intellectual, physical, and social interests. The narrowing of their identity to that of "mother" was disturbing, as they
felt they were losing self-identities that they valued and wanted
to maintain.

Over time, women began to perceive their children as
Obstacles, disruptive elements in their lives (Table 7). While
some mothers viewed the child as a slight nuisance, others felt

the child obstructed major life goals. These latter women felt stymied, overwhelmed, and harassed. Feelings of anger and resentment alternated with feelings of guilt and remorse over their inappropriate attitudes on parenting. As mothers, they experienced strong emotions, which vacillated from pride and love to resentment and anger.

Husbands were confused by their wives' strong vacillating emotions and unpredictable behavior. They began to feel their wives were cold and not nurturing enough and criticized their management of the children. The couples thus began to experience a great deal of conflict over child rearing.

Couples were never able to resolve their different interpretations of marriage and family life. Perhaps women failed to communicate the intensity of their distress with their husbands, or maybe men failed to receive and accept these messages. These messages may have threatened men because women appeared to be deviating from a valued maternal role; also, they created demands on men to assume more responsibilities with the children. Generally these men were involved in developing their careers and were not willing to reorganize their commitments and priorities.

In all ten families the father ultimately gained custody. In their experience of the legal process two women in the Fractured Family pattern contested custody but were not successful in gaining support for themselves. (See "Fractured Families," in Chapter Three, for a more detailed discussion of this process.) In the other eight families, women voluntarily relinquished custody to their husbands.

While paths to this end varied, one feature was common in all eight families: The woman did not leave the family suddenly but gradually relinquished responsibility for the children over a period of time. The family was prepared for the woman's departure in several ways. First, she gradually attained greater emotional and physical distance as she worked longer hours and was absent more often from the home. The burden of care gradually shifted to the father. By the time of the separation, the children related to the father as the primary parent. Some families experienced "rehearsals" of her departure. She talked about her plans to leave and, in some cases, actually left for a short time and then returned. Although this temporary leave reflected the woman's ambivalence and was not set up as an attempt to prepare the family for her departure, it did give the family a trial period to live alone and gain confidence in their ability to manage the household. In one family, the wife actually worked out many details in advance. She wanted a divorce but knew her husband would not leave the home. Feeling that departure would be a very big step for both her and the family, she sought help from an agency that aided people in "problem solving." Her counselor asked her many questions and gave her "homework," which included finding solutions to some of the practical problems of turning over management of the home to her husband. She prepared him for the responsibilities of shopping, preparing meals, and doing the laundry. She also employed a college student to assist with housework and meals. In this way she was eventually able to leave, feeling the household was under control and she was not simply abandoning her family.

Not all women ended the marriage by moving out of the house and away from the family. Three women began the separation period by remaining in the house with the children. However, after very brief periods, they decided, for various reasons, to move away and asked the father to come back and live with the children.

The women's greatest difficulty was accepting the legitimacy of their move away from the children. They felt they "should" have custody of the children; especially with young children, they reasoned that the mother should be the primary parent. During the years and months prior to the separation, they wrestled with this question. Finally, they recognized that in spite of cultural norms, their husbands, for a variety of reasons, were more effective parents. Sheryl recalled her feelings:

Sheryl: For a while there was a lot of uncertainty. Marc always felt that he wanted custody. I felt for awhile that I *should* want custody . . . If I were any kind of a woman, I really should want it; what would people think if I didn't? Psychologically speaking, it was probably better for Jeffrey to be with his mother; he was about four at the time. And so I thought at first that . . . if we had to decide which of us would get physical custody, that I should ask for it. But finally, I came to the conclusion that I was really *not* at all that comfortable having Jeffrey around, that I resented a great deal of the pressures that were on me when he was around. That was not good for Jeffrey, and it was not good for me or for our eventual relationship. I was able finally to give custody to Marc quite voluntarily.

The issue of which parent was the more "effective" with the child was often a painful one for these women. As Sheryl indicated, she realized she was not comfortable with Jeffrey. He was much more relaxed and "natural" with his father than he was with her. He seemed to respond to Marc and was happier at his home than with her. She wanted her child to choose and prefer her as a parent, but she also knew she could not expect him to prefer a parent who was less attentive and demonstrative.

For some women, acknowledging the father as the more effective parent and leaving the children in his care involved struggles with their own identity as women. Although women found it difficult to cope with and discuss their feelings about themselves as mothers, they could readily discuss pragmatic reasons for their decisions on custody. They were not secure financially. Most of them either did not have careers or were just in the process of establishing themselves. They feared the strain of combining work, family responsibilities, and the physical upkeep of the family home. Knowing their children were settled and secure in the home, they did not want to uproot them and move them to a smaller house or apartment. By refusing to move and by demonstrating their ability to maintain a home for the children, the men gained much in their move toward custody. In many families, maintenance of the family home proved to be an important factor in determining custody.

Although only a few women were articulate about the relation between the mothering role and their own identity as females, all women were conscious of the real financial stresses of single parenthood. Ultimately, the public reasons for their private choices were voiced in these terms: they could not financially or physically manage the home, the family, and a new career. Their husbands, who were more financially and occupationally secure, were in better positions to manage the load.

Throughout the separation period, other interpretations similarly minimized the psychological and social impact of their decisions. Women invariably interpreted their actions as "temporary." They moved out of the house for a "trial separation." Gail had her children with her but asked her husband to take them for a trial period of three months. At the end of the three months, she made no effort to have the children return to her. Women also kept arrangements open-ended by fantasizing a reversal of decisions in the future. Ann Marie, who lived in a small apartment, discussed the possibility of finding a larger place if her children should come to live with her. Barbara planned to have the children with her more after she completed night school classes. Maria and Vic agreed that the roles might be reversed in the future if she returned to the home and the children and he moved out.

Agreements between the husband and wife tended, therefore, to stress the flexibility and the temporary nature of the arrangements. Privately, however, men felt the arrangements would not change. Eventually the men initiated legal termination of the marriage. This move aroused anxiety for the women, because legal specifications of the custodial arrangements appeared more permanent. When men initiated the legal proceedings, women tended to avoid them and left the legal negotiations to their husbands, or they made some slight gesture toward regaining custody of the children. For example, Maria, who had been away from the home for over two years, asked for custody of two of the four children when her husband filed for dissolution. However, she did not fight hard for the children and readily accepted the conciliation court's judgment awarding custody to the father. Men recognized the social pressures their wives were facing and interpreted these gestures as "face-saving." They found that their best strategy was simply to avoid confrontation and give their wives as much time as possible. They refused to rush the legal proceedings, realizing that time would both help their wives feel more comfortable with the situation and enable them to establish their own record as capable fathers.

Most of these families did not contest custody, but in cases in which it was contested, it appeared that all participants knew the outcome from the beginning. In reality, the legal contest was little more than a ritual that allowed the woman an opportunity to demonstrate before the community her maternal intentions and desires. The necessity for such a ritual attested both to the strength of the social pressures directed against these women and to their own ambivalence.

Women did not adjust easily to this period of separation from their families. They missed their children and the stability and security of family life. It was an intense period of readjustment, provoking very strong emotional reactions of fear, loneliness, and guilt, as well as relief. Ann Marie described how "crazy" she felt:

Ann Marie: I think I was a little crazy at the time [laughs]. It was like starting everything all over again. I had no friends because my married friends were not seeing me. My mother and father didn't stop speaking to me, but they didn't have much to say to me. They just felt I was mentally deranged [laughs] or going through a phase or whatever you want to call it. They thought all this would pass and I would come to my senses and go home . . . I was depressed a lot. I don't think I ever felt guilty.

Most of these women found they had to establish new support systems. Old friends, who could not understand their "selfish" behavior, gradually stopped calling and seeing them. Since it is not common for women to leave their families, most of the women did not know any other mothers who had left their children. Only one woman had a friend who had made a similar decision. She found her friendship and advice most helpful. Sheryl felt it would have been a real advantage to have this support.

Interviewer: Do you think it would have helped to have some contact with women who did not have custody?

Sheryl: Distinctly so, just being able to talk to someone and maybe discover that you could be a woman and human being and have made this decision. It would have been easier for me to make this decision.

Children's responses to their mothers' move varied greatly from one family to another. In most cases the mother's departure did not appear to affect the child's social behavior or academic performance. Younger children sometimes played the role of peacemaker, trying to get their parents to resume living together. They also voiced fear that their own behavior had caused their mother to leave; Sheryl noted how her young son was on his "best behavior" with her because he feared she would reject him. His visits were, therefore, not relaxed but were restricted and tense. Verbal assurances to the child and attempts to relieve him of guilt were not very effective. In two families with teenage girls, the girls temporarily distanced themselves emotionally from their mothers and sought out substitute women in the community as confidants and friends. Teenage boys, though angry with their mother for leaving, tended to maintain contact with her. Although the reaction of the child varied according to sex and age, the mother's decision to leave was not based on this factor. All ages from infants to teenagers and both sexes were represented in these families. In the interviews, the women clearly indicated that their departure was not precipitated by their children or by their children's behavior; rather, these women were rejecting a *role* that they had found rigid and untenable. They experienced the parenting and marital roles as too confining and ultimately rejected both their husband's attempts to control their behavior and social pressures to conform.

The Child as Caretaker: Split Parenting

The primary identifying characteristic of Split Parenting was the child's assumption of a *Caretaker* role for the parent perceived as "victim," or loser, within the marriage. In these six families, an imbalance of power existed between the husband and wife. Two different types of Caretaking relationships were associated with two marital patterns: in three Doll's House Marriages, women had gained power in the marriage, and children were protective of the father, who appeared to be the victim. In three Fractured Families, men dominated the relationship, and children perceived the mother as the loser.

In the three Doll's House families, the children identified the mother as the parent who had caused the divorce. Women in these families appeared to be quite effective parents. They expressed warm, affectionate attitudes toward their children and were confident in their ability to discipline and manage the children. Their children, however, were protective and solicitous of their fathers, whom they perceived as "losers" in the marital struggle.

In varying degrees these children assumed the role of Caretaker. A reversal of the normal parent/child relationship occurred as the father assumed a child's role in seeking nurturance and support and the child attempted to play the parenting role of protecting and nurturing. Frequently these children felt sorry for fathers, who they felt had been "pushed" out of the home. Doris's son worried about his father's financial needs, and when Glen complained about not having enough money, the child attempted to give him his piggy bank. Again, when Glen told his son that the son had better tools than he had ever had as a child, the boy tried to give him the tools.

Men, who were struggling with serious problems at that point in their lives, found pleasure in their children's attachments and encouraged their solicitations. Two of the three men were unemployed, and all three were very distressed with their wives' leaving the marriage. They had little energy or desire to attend to the children's needs. Adult needs gained priority in the relationship, and the child's needs tended to be suppressed by the intensity of the parent's demands.

Children's awareness and acceptance of this reversal of roles varied greatly. Boys did not appear to resent their father's appeal to them, but teenage girls were very keenly aware of the demands their father was placing on them and resented the reversal of roles. Nancy recalled:

Interviewer: What kinds of feelings were they expressing at that time?

Nancy: Joan moved out; she was very, very angry with her father, because he wasn't listening to what anybody was saying. He wasn't taking any responsibility for the break at all. It was all my fault . . . The other two were very ambivalent about leaving. I think they felt guilty about leaving Greg . . . They were with him six months, and he really blew it. He just fell apart . . . He got more and more depressed. He was the child and they were the parents. Joan said, "I'm tired of being a mother to him. I want to be his daughter. I want him to be a father to me."

Within these three families the child often played a *Stabilizer* role for the mother. These women remained very involved with their children and continued to express their concern for them. They felt their children were in some ways trying to continue the same role that they, as wives, had just abandoned. Arlene felt some guilt leaving her son with this role:

Arlene: Chris is sort of an angry young man right now. He chose to go with his father. I think he summarized it when he told a friend of mine that Mom has all the breaks and Dad doesn't have anyone. Michael is willing to be rescued by a thirteen-year-old. And Chris felt compelled to do the rescuing . . . I feel Chris's problem right now is being responsible for his father, and it's an overwhelming responsibility for a kid that age. I feel I kind of dropped my responsibility on Chris when I moved out. I feel guilty about that.

Arlene and Doris both felt they needed to protect their children from some knowledge about the marriage. They therefore did not explain their reasons for wanting a divorce and did not tell them about their father's problems. For example, Arlene did not tell her teenage son the father had threatened to commit suicide. She did not want to worry him, and she also wanted to protect his image of the father. In the absence of this and similar information, he filled in the reasons for the divorce as the "mother's need to be her own person":

Arlene: The last few months I was remiss with Chris in that I didn't tell him many things. When Michael was going through all this strife and turmoil, I tried to keep it low-key and not let him realize how shaky things were, by being very cool about it, like it would go away. And meantime Chris was really filling his head with a lot of stuff like "Mom has to be her own person. We've got to sit back and let Mom do her own thing." . . . I don't know how much he knew, but I failed him. I said, "Your dad is tired. And he needs a rest." And I didn't tell him that his father had threatened to blow his brains out. I didn't feel he needed that extra pressure. However, not knowing is sometimes more upsetting than knowing what the problem is.

Again, the family with the teenage girls was a little different. The girls were much more aware of tensions within the marriage and episodes leading up to the divorce. Further, they resented the way their father controlled their mother, and they told her she had to do something:

Nancy: Before our trip to Europe, Joan said, "If you don't do something, if you don't leave, I'm going to leave. You've got to do something. Why are you tolerating the situation? Why are you allowing this to happen to yourself?" . . . When we were in Europe, Beth said the same thing to me. The kids were very supportive. They realized what was going on.

Differences in the male and female children's responses to their parents' divorces were not due entirely, however, to a difference in the *amount* of information they had on the marital problems. Although the boys seemed to have less information, they also seemed to *perceive* less information about their father's behavior. Even though, for example, Chris saw his father in a rage and perceived that he might beat his mother, and knew his father repeatedly lost jobs, he refused to hold his father equally responsible for the marital problems and insisted they were due to his mother's need for personal development and her inexcusable abandonment of the family. Thus, he discounted messages that would have required him to perceive his father in a different perspective.

The identification and the alliance of the male teenager with the father were similar to the alliances formed between fathers and sons in some Uncommitted Parenting families. These family patterns were very different, however, because the mothers handled the children's reactions differently. Women in the Split Parenting group shielded their children from knowledge that would have caused difficulty in the son's identification with his father. Rather than try to gain the children's allegiance through exposure of their mate's inadequacies, they supported the child's relationship with the father. They absorbed their children's anger in the hope that it would subside with time. They felt assured of a continuing close relationship with their children and perceived the children's responses at the time of the divorce as intense but temporary responses of anger and hurt. They therefore continued in a nurturing, supportive role; eventually the children began to move back again into a closer relationship with their mothers.

Within the three Fractured Families in the Split Parenting group, the child perceived the *mother* as the less powerful parent. Relationships between children and parents were very complicated. All but one of the children were school-age males; they identified with their father and imitated his behavior, but they had a close relationship with the mother. The mothers were very nurturing and warm in their relationships with their children but were not confident in their ability to manage and discipline them (Table 6). Conversely, fathers in this group did not appear to be very nurturing but were quite competent in managing their children. Thus, the child was split between one parent who gave him the love and emotional support he needed and another parent who was able to discipline him and structure his life.

A wide imbalance in power within the marriage contributed to this split in parenting effectiveness. Early in the family life, mothers were more involved parents and were probably more effective with the children. They wanted children and responded positively to the birth of the child.

In contrast, men were minimally involved with the children. Ann, the mother of two boys, said:

Ann: I think he wanted boys. Everybody says he would have been crazy about a little girl. On Jim's part, maybe it would have been a good idea because he would have shown more emotion, affection. Boys do not cry, and boys do not sit in Daddy's lap and cuddle.

As the boys became school age, they became more difficult to manage. They began to act aggressively in the classroom, and parents received complaints from teachers, who had difficulty handling them. At home these boys became abusive toward their mother and refused to follow her rules. While this aggressiveness may have stemmed from a variety of causes, two mothers perceived it as associated with the father's behavior.

The men in these three families were quite aggressive. They displayed their anger by yelling, pounding walls, and breaking furniture. There was no indication that they were physically abusive toward their wives. However, they spanked their children rather severely with their hands and belts when they felt they had misbehaved. In addition, children observed their fathers' anger and abusive attitudes toward their mothers. Cynthia recalled her son's reactions to these episodes:

Cynthia: He would yell at me in front of Kevin, and Kevin would get very quiet. I can remember one time

when he was eighteen months old and sitting in
his high chair. Matt was yelling, and Kevin's eyes
got this big . . . I would see it coming, and I knew
he was upset with me or with Kevin, and I would
say, "Let's go talk about this in the bedroom.
Kevin's sitting here."

Interviewer: What did Kevin do, then, when he was old enough
to understand more?

Cynthia: He would be very naughty with me and repeat to
me what he heard his father say.

Women felt their children learned to imitate their fathers.
They observed behaviors in their young sons that were very
similar to the father's behaviors:

Interviewer: I understand that you and your husband had disagreements on the way the child should be han-
dled.

Cynthia: Yes, that's true.

Interviewer: How would Kevin respond to these disagreements?

Cynthia: Oh, he would be naughty and nasty toward me
. . . Some of the words that he used against me in
anger were words that Matt had used two days
before against me, and so I could just see him
picking this up from his dad.

Interviewer: Was Matt aware of this?

Cynthia: I tried to talk with him about this, but it didn't
get through.

Women, who were suffering the pain of a dissolving marriage, who now perceived their sons were treating them similarly to their husbands, became very angry with these children:

Cynthia: I would just yell at him. I was kind of nasty verbally with Kevin, which I am ashamed of now.

Interviewer: Did you punish him, then, like spank him?

Cynthia: Oh, yes. I found myself yelling at him and not

beating him, but spanking him hard. It frightened me, very much sometimes. I guess I always thought I should not vent my anger at this child.

Cynthia and Ann felt very guilty about their loss of control with the children:

Ann:	They run circles around me.
Interviewer:	What do you do when they do that?
Ann:	[Sighs] Well, I spank them. Since the divorce I have had a lot of problems with guilt feelings [tears, half crying]. I spank them and then love them. I spank them because they don't listen. I get very frustrated because David doesn't listen.

Women's feelings of love for their children alternated with their feelings of anger and frustration. During the separation period, the emotions expressed by both the children and their mothers became very intense.

The children in these three families lived with their fathers, who were judged more effective in managing them. The children, however, appeared very ambivalent about their placement. Male children who identified with their father and imitated his behavior were also dependent on their mother for nurturance. Although they behaved better with their fathers, they did not confide in them or seek comfort from them. They sought comfort from their mothers and were solicitous and protective of them. Their behavior suggested ambivalence and confusion. At times they assumed the role of Caretaker for their mother; at other times, they displayed rebellious, aggressive behaviors.

Thus, within both the Doll's House and Fractured Families in this parenting group, the children, especially males, were torn in their loyalties to their parents. Their perceptions of one parent as victim aroused tender feelings of protectiveness. Parent/child relationships became particularly complicated when the child perceived the opposite-sex parent as victim and felt solicitous of this parent but also identified with and imitated the behavior of the same-sex parent. Within these families, relationships between the victim parent and child were particularly intense and fraught with conflicting emotions. In Split Parenting families, custody of children remained a problem for both parents and children. The intense emotional conflicts in loyalty may quite possibly signal some emotional difficulties for these children in future years.

In summary, children played a variety of roles in these separating families. These roles, which were related to the way the husband and wife exercised power in their relationship, had varying consequences for the children. The Stabilizer role was found among those families in which the husband and wife had a relatively egalitarian relationship. They were able to share parenting, and consequently the children continued to enjoy the support of both parents. Compared with others, these children were probably the least disturbed by the divorce. In two other patterns—Maternal and Paternal Parenting—children were similarly protected by a strong, stable relationship with one parent. The second parent, while less involved in the day-to-day management of the children, continued to care for them and contributed some support and attention. Distress at the time of separation was minimized as these couples achieved agreement on the issue of custody. Without any contest, they were able to recognize one parent as more dominant and granted that parent physical and legal custody. Children were thus kept in a stable environment and did not have to choose between two competing parents.

The most difficult situations for the children were obviously the Uncommitted and Split Parenting patterns, in which children were torn in their loyalties between two warring parents. In the Uncommitted Parenting families, the husband's use of punitive power and the couple's inability to plan for or control their family life created an environment charged with tension and conflict. Children had little emotional security with either parent and became Hostages or pawns in the marital battle. In the last pattern, Split Parenting, children suffered emotional conflicts because of the way they were split between two parents. An imbalance or shift in marital power made one parent appear as the loser. Children were torn between assuming a Caretaking, protective role for this parent and living with the second parent, who in some cases was stronger and more capable of nurturing and managing the child. In these families the split between the husband and wife was reflected in a split within the child. The child, reflecting inner confusion and ambivalence, alternated between loving expressions of fierce loyalty and angry acts of rebellion. In these last two family groups, the marital tensions and hostility became lodged in the child, and the child became the battlefield.

7

The Impact
of Divorce on Children

Early in the book I described
two stereotypes of women who do not have custody of their
children—the "unfit mother" and the "liberated woman." The
"unfit mother" raises images of a woman who physically or
emotionally neglects her children because she is an alcoholic,
an addict, mentally ill, or sexually promiscuous. The "liberated
woman," in contrast, may be competent but is too selfish to
care for her children; she abandons all family responsibilities to
seek personal fulfillment.

These stereotypes are caricatures that distort and over-
simplify family life. Furthermore, they place responsibility for
family outcomes on one person only—the woman—and completely ignore the attitudes and behaviors of other family members that may contribute to this outcome. For example, these
stereotypes tell us nothing about the husband's behaviors and
the impact he has on his wife and children. In addition, they

suggest children are victims or passive recipients of their mother's behavior.

In Chapters Three through Six, I described interaction within six types of families. Families created certain styles of interaction, which shaped the way they lived together and the way they separated. Interactions were complex and always changing, never simple or static. Ultimately, the approach to separation and divorce was shaped not by one family member but by all family members, including the children.

In my interpretations of family life, I have made certain theoretical assumptions, which I will discuss more fully in this chapter. These assumptions are as follows: Marriage is an interactive process. Over the years, couples create meaning, or a shared history, as they interact with each other. Their interaction is shaped by three important elements: power, status, and love. These elements do not remain constant but change in response to certain events within the family's history. For example, the birth of a child, a new job, unemployment, or even a change in ties with family and friends can change each partner's feelings of love, or the relative status or power he or she possesses within the relationship.

Finally, these marital processes affect the children; marital politics shapes the child's experiences within the family. The child's behaviors, in turn, influence the husband's and wife's relationship.

Using examples from the lives of these forty men and women, I will describe these family processes more fully in this chapter. I will also discuss the work of other social scientists whose interpretations of family life may be similar to or different from my perspectives.

Marriage: The Interactive Process of Creating Meaning

In my interpretation of marriage, I have used Berger and Kellner's definition of marriage as "an essential relationship which creates meaning and order for two individuals" (1979, p. 308). When men and women marry, they come together with unshared past histories. As they live together over the years, they construct a new shared biography, or history, with common meanings. They create this common biography by interacting with and responding to each other.

The simplest, most basic behaviors may be called "gestures." Gestures, which may be either verbal or nonverbal, are "behaviors that can be assigned some meaning by both persons" (Turner, 1970, p. 21). The emphasis here is on meaning—individuals do not simply react to each other's behaviors. They interpret or define each other's actions and base their responses on the meanings they attach to these actions.

In each of the six marital patterns described in this book, husbands and wives created unique interactional styles by using certain sequences of gestures. For example, Fragile Bond couples withdrew from each other; they separated their work roles and withheld themselves emotionally. In the Stalemate marriages, the male used a similar gesture of withdrawal and separated himself from his wife, but the wife responded differently. Unhappy with his withdrawal, she alternately appealed to him for attention and love and attacked him for his indifference. Because the women responded so differently to the men's gestures of avoidance, these two types of marriages assumed very different shapes and were undoubtedly experienced quite differently by the couples themselves.

Power: The Formation of Rules and Definitions

As couples live together, they create rules or norms defining behaviors; some behaviors are regarded as acceptable while others are less acceptable. Again, in the Fragile Bond marriages, couples tacitly accepted the rule that it is better to leave than to fight. When any conflict emerged, one partner simply left the house; the couple refused to "fight it out" and did not question each other's right to withdraw from the situation. In other marriages, leaving may be against the rules, and partners may follow other strategies in dealing with conflict.

Couples regulate their emotions as well as their behaviors. They create "feeling rules" about which emotions are appropriate and the acceptable means for expressing these emotions.

They then learn to manage their emotions to conform to those feeling rules (Hochschild, 1979). Ralph, for example, wanted to spend some time with his wife on Sunday afternoons. He resented the frequent interruptions from the children but found it difficult to express this resentment. He and his wife had established an "open house" that was child-oriented. The couple catered to the children's needs, and Ralph learned to manage his feelings of resentment. Perhaps he was permitted to complain mildly about the children's intrusions, but he was not expected to display a more intense anger.

Couples are seldom able to identify the rules that regulate their behaviors and emotions. These rules exist as covert boundaries outlining appropriate ranges of behaviors. While codes on behavior may be a little more noticeable to the husband and wife, rules about emotions are particularly difficult to identify. Their invisibility, however, does not diminish their effectiveness. On the contrary, the lack of visibility makes these rules even more binding. In fact, as individuals develop greater awareness, they may be more successful not only in changing rules but in creating rules in their favor.

In any marriage, the key issue eventually becomes: Which partner will establish rules for behaving and feeling? Even more important, which partner will have more power to interpret situations and define appropriate responses? In everyday life, couples confront many ambiguous situations, which may be perceived in a variety of ways. Partners may disagree in their interpretations of these situations and the behaviors they consider appropriate. Through an interactive process, the couple ascribes some meaning to the event and responds to it. The partner who can successfully control this process of defining both the situation and the appropriate behaviors has a distinct advantage in being able to channel the marriage in directions more rewarding and satisfying to him or her. Power, or the ability to control and dominate the relationship, originates in this act of defining. Although it may at times also involve a more direct and even brutal imposition of one's will on another, the most effective power may exist simply in this subtle ability to control meanings, definitions, and rules in the relationship.

Two examples illustrate how power is maintained by controlling the definitions of events. Kevin was able to talk his wife into having an abortion. He did this by defining their situation in such a way that Virginia would see that having a baby was not appropriate. It would create disruption in their plans for school and work. Virginia "bought" his explanation, accommodated to his wishes, and had an abortion. She also emotionally managed any feelings of sadness, anger, or guilt she may have had about this experience. Giving in to her husband's definitions required not only following a certain sequence of behaviors but overriding and suppressing some emotional responses.

Denise, enraged when her husband arrived home at 5:00 A.M. from an office party, overturned the coffee table and broke it. He told her she was crazy and threatened to have her committed. The next day she felt guilty for breaking the table and was grateful to him for not telling anyone. At other times in the marriage Jack physically assaulted her. In each situation, Denise accepted Jack's interpretation. She was crazy for breaking the table, she provoked him to beat her. As she accepted his interpretations, she realigned her emotions. Instead of being angry with him, she felt guilty and was contrite. Jack was thus able to channel the interaction in such a way that he did not have to confront her anger or explain his own behavior.

Norms and expectations within the larger society may also affect the couple's creation of rules on behavior and emotions. Social expectations assume some behaviors and emotions are appropriate to a particular situation, while others are not. For example, couples are expected to experience pride and joy on the birth of their first child. Sheryl knew she did not want a child; she felt an "inner terror" over the prospect of having a child, but she did not disclose this feeling to anyone because it struck her as "dreadful and unspeakable." If people knew she felt this way, what would they think of her?

Couples thus experience some constraints; they are bound to keep both their behaviors and emotional expressions within a socially acceptable range. In addition, one partner within the marriage may have less control over the process of defining situations and may thus have to conform more frequently to the rules established by the other. Again, conformity means not only behaving appropriately but feeling appropriately. This requires, at times, a repression or realignment of one's emotions. The partner with less power must work a little harder to accommodate emotionally and manage these feelings.

Status and Love in Marriage

Power within the marriage is closely related to two other elements: love and status. Love is a strong emotional attachment; it includes both sexual desire and tenderness. Through sharing experiences, couples create emotional bonds and depend on each other for support. Status defines the position of two persons relative to each other in marriage. An individual with high status is perceived favorably by the other and is able to gain voluntary compliance from the partner (Kemper, 1978, p. 30). Conversely, persons with low status are regarded less highly by mates; they are less able to gain voluntary compliance and may need to rely more on coercion to gain their objectives. Thus, *status* refers to the relative position of the partners and the consequent ease with which they are able to elicit desired responses from each other.

Marital Changes in Status: "Falling Out of Love." In the early stages of a love relationship, partners generally grant each other a high status and willingly meet each other's needs. High-status relationships, are, however, difficult to sustain. As the couple live together, each is exposed to undesirable behaviors or characteristics in the spouse. Moreover, the standards on which they based their early relationship may have been transient. The man who falls in love with a woman because she is beautiful may find it difficult to retain that attraction as her beauty fades. Or a woman who values her husband because he is attentive becomes disturbed when he turns most of his attention to his business.

The process by which lovers move from high status to low status is called, in colloquial terms, "falling out of love" (Kemper, 1978). Couples respond differently to this process. Some may be able to shed their romantic idealizations and develop a deeper level of trust and caring for each other. Like all couples, they lose status in the sense that their faults and defects are exposed to each other, but they gain a new status level as they discover other, more enduring, attractive qualities in each other. They may eventually develop a deeper love based on more realistic expectations.

Undoubtedly, some couples are able to achieve this more enduring love. For others, the relationship deteriorates as they become intimate. "Falling out of love" ultimately leads to greater alienation, separation, and finally divorce. This process, which is exemplified in the families in this study, will be described in the following paragraphs.

Early in their relationships, these couples were willing to comply with each other's wishes, and their gestures, therefore, could be subtle, positive, and rewarding. As partners lost status with each other, they either turned from each other and avoided the relationship or attempted to coerce the partner into desired responses. Behaviors thus became more intense, punitive, and threatening.

Male and Female Differences in Loss of Status. Although the process of falling out of love may be similar for women and men, and both partners may eventually occupy a lower status with each other, the woman's status is more vulnerable and more subject to threat of reduction. Both the structure of the larger society and the process within marriage contribute to an early and often rapid decline in status for women.

First, as a group, women enjoy less status in our society. Early in a love relationship, a man believes his loved one is a very special woman; she is "more than" other women and enjoys equal or almost equal status with him because she is his special woman. As the relationship continues, she slips back into the status of being more like other women or "just" a woman: "Although falling in love may create a surge of egalitarianism or even reversal of adjudged superiority, the attenuation or loss of the grounds for this unwontedly high status reduces the woman to her former, lesser status. Although she may still command higher status from her husband (or lover) than do other women, she is after all *just* a woman and partakes therefore in the generally lower status of women" (Kemper, 1978, p. 321).

Second, an individual woman's status is reduced as she becomes more dependent on men economically and socially as well as psychologically. Need for the partner's support depends partly on the extensiveness of support received from others outside the home. Contacts with other persons through work, friendships, and outside interests widen the base of social and emotional support. Thus, the partner with the wider base of external resources requires less support. Again, this condition in general favors men and makes the woman's situation more difficult. Particularly in traditional marital roles, women discover that their base of support diminishes when they become housewives and focus their attention on the home, thereby reducing contacts with persons outside the home. They consequently become more dependent on their husbands for supplying their needs.

In summary, women, particularly in more traditional marriages, struggle with both a general loss in status because of their membership in a devalued class and a greater dependency created by a reduced base for support outside the marriage. A woman may experience this withdrawal of status in innumerable ways; she realizes she is becoming less important to her husband as he fails to listen to her or ignores her needs and desires in lovemaking. She experiences this withdrawal of status as a loss; the fact that it happens gradually over a period of years does not diminish its impact or make it less disturbing (Kemper, 1978, p. 321).

Emotional Responses to Romantic Love and Loss of Status. The woman's loss of status within the marriage is concealed by the ideology of romantic love. Romantic love is a passionate, intense love, in which the loved one is perceived as having attributes valued by the lover. To continue this level of intense love, the loved one must continue to exhibit the desired qualities. This often requires a process of idealization, in which the loved one is granted desirable qualities, which, in fact, he or she may not have; less desirable qualities may be ignored or excused.

Financially and emotionally dependent women are most apt to idealize their partners. As seen in Chapter Three, traditional women in Fractured Families were more dependent on their mates. Because loss of the relationship was so threatening to them, they continued to idealize their husbands in spite of evidence clearly indicating undesirable characteristics or behaviors. For example, Denise clung to the idea that Jack was faithful to her, in spite of overwhelming evidence of his love affairs.

Idealization and clinging to an image of romantic love affects both partners. Initially, the husband may be flattered by his wife's positive images of him, but over time these images become burdensome. Jack, for example, may eventually feel guilty because he has too much power in the relationship. Denise is too eager to accept explanations from him that will sustain his idealized image. Consequently, he is given too much power and wins too often. Quite possibly, he may also experience some shame as he realizes that he is not as good, and can never be as good, as she believes him to be. Kemper (1978, p. 62) suggests that the idealized partner may turn shame into hostility toward the other for demanding continuation of an impossible image. Living on a pedestal is not only uncomfortable but invites contempt and anger.

For the woman, the consequences may be even more distressing. As she feels a withdrawal of status by her husband, she becomes depressed and anxious. Later, when the illusions of romantic love can no longer be retained, she feels shame for having trusted and for being deceived.

Thus, the ideology of romantic love encourages maintenance of intense bonds that can be sustained only through idealization and denial of reality. A financially and socially dependent woman needs her husband's emotional commitment to keep him secured to the family. It is her security against loss, but to the man, it may feel like bondage, a claim made on him that he does not wish to honor. Ultimately, both partners are embittered as they realize their images of love bind them together in a relationship devoid of real tenderness.

Although women are generally more dependent on the marriage and will, therefore, seek more frequently to maintain it through appeals to love, it is possible for the situation to be reversed. Men in the Doll's House families appeared more emotionally dependent on the marriage. They expected their wives to reciprocate an emotional commitment. When love was not returned and their relative status within the marriage was reduced, they responded with similar reactions of depression and anger.

These emotional responses are not sex-linked but are associated with the painful loss of status in a valued relationship. Both men and women who lost status in their marriage became depressed. This depression was a reaction to their loss and an expression of longing for the benefits and rewards that were withdrawn. While both sexes may react similarly, women may suffer from depression more than men because they more often experience a loss of status in their intimate relationships.

Power and the Egalitarian Marriage

I suggested earlier that status, or the position of spouses relative to each other, is seldom equal. Women's status is generally lower, and men can more easily dominate and control the relationship.

It may, of course, be argued that in recent years women have gained some ground in their struggle for equality. They now have more opportunity for occupational advancement and financial success, which, in turn, may translate into a greater leverage, or bargaining power, within marriage.

Was there any evidence of this movement toward egalitarian relationships among the families in this study? How did these families compare on this dimension of power?

The six patterns differed greatly in their distribution of power between husband and wife. If they were to be placed on a continuum with husband-dominant families on one end and wife-dominant families on the other, the Fractured Families would be most characteristic of husband-dominant families. Raven, Centers, and Rodrigues (1975) identified six bases of power: legitimate, referent, expert, informational, reward, and coercive. On all six bases of power, these husbands were more dominant. Since these families followed a traditional ideology, husbands were granted more authority, or legitimate power. If wives identified with their husbands, as some appeared to do, men were high on referent power. They had both expert and informational power, as they had more knowledge of the world outside the marriage and more skill in coping with that world. Men also controlled the administration of rewards and punishments; for example, they controlled money and were able to allocate or withhold this resource. They also used coercive power against family members, children as well as wives, to gain compliance. Of all six patterns, these families appeared to be the most clearly husband-dominant in both ideology and behavior.

Perhaps the Doll's House families could be placed on the wife-dominant end of the continuum. However, these families were not wife-dominant in the sense that women characteristically dominated the marriage from beginning to end. Rather, the women in these families *resisted* the husband's dominance; the pattern appeared to become more wife-dominant only toward the end of the marriage. These marriages began in fairly traditional ways, following conventional modes for division of labor. Women followed certain structural arrangements that gave the man's needs priority. For example, they placed his career ahead of their own; they worked so he could finish medical or graduate school. They allowed him to persuade them in matters of family planning and child rearing.

At a critical point within the marriage, women questioned this pattern and sought to change it. In the years immediately preceding the separation, a reversal of power occurred in the marriage as women gained access to resources outside the marriage and became more skillful in negotiating for what they needed within the marriage. The men correspondingly reduced their access to other resources and were less able to negotiate within the marriage.

Thus, these families were not wife-dominated in the sense that the woman controlled the relationship from beginning to end. She asserted herself only toward the end of the marriage. It was this assertion and resistance to husband dominance that precipitated the end of the marriage.

The Unformed Families may also be termed wife-dominant. Perhaps these marriages were never male-dominated because women showed a lack of bonding and commitment to the marriage. However, these marriages were very short-lived. Thus, within this group of forty families, the two patterns that could be termed "wife-dominant" had very short life spans.

In the middle of the scale may be placed the Perfect Model families, which appeared quite egalitarian. The partners in these marriages were more equally balanced in resources. At least by the end of the marriage, women had access to profitable and satisfying employment. They had high levels of education and secure positions with good salaries. They did not identify with their husbands or bestow on them the referent power found in more traditional families. Furthermore, couples were young and were more committed to contemporary ideals of marriage. Both the husband and wife would probably deny that the husband *should* have authority within the marriage. These families, then, epitomized the ideal in their acceptance of an egalitarian ideology, their equality in work, and their approach to negotiation and dialogue within the marriage.

However, I would argue that these marriages were more successful in creating the *illusion* of equality than the *substance*. Flexibility of gestures contributed to an appearance of negotiation, but outcomes were tilted in the husband's favor, and he was characteristically favored in both long- and short-term decisions. For example, even though both the husband and wife had careers, when it came to questions of mobility or time allowed in the daily schedule, his work was given precedence. He "helped" in the house when it was convenient for him, but household tasks and child rearing were still her primary responsibility. Her work was useful and produced income needed for the family budget, but it was still not as interesting or significant as his. In public her feminist views were accepted as ideologically correct, but in their own private dialogues, he dismissed them as trivial and boring. Sexually, he accepted her "right" to the satisfaction of orgasm but complained about her needs and interpreted them as a demand for performance that detracted from his own pleasure.

Since the process of powering in these marriages stressed dialogue, persuasion rather than coercion, negotiation rather than authoritarian decision making, they appeared quite egalitarian. But a closer examination of the family process quite clearly indicates that the husband's wishes were given priority. The imbalance of power was concealed and softened by an ideological commitment to equality and a process of negotiation that appeared democratic.

Evolution of the marriage is important, therefore, in understanding family politics. Within these families husband-dominant marriages were able to sustain a long life, but wife-dominant or even clearly egalitarian patterns could not be sustained as long. They more characteristically represented a *stage* in the evolution of marriage, rather than a long-term, well-established pattern.

Impact of Marital Politics on the Child's Experience of Divorce

Control and domination are very important issues in any relationship. Shifts in power and status have an impact not only on the marriage but also on the way the couple approaches divorce. But does the politics of the marriage have any impact on children? How do they respond to shifts in marital power? More specifically, does the particular marital pattern affect the way children experience the divorce?

Using findings from other studies, clinical observations, and data from this research study, I will show that the politics of the marriage does affect the children and shapes their experiences during the period of separation and divorce. In particular, marital patterns involving a severe imbalance in power have a profoundly disturbing impact on children. Marital patterns involving a more short-term shift in power also elicit a response from children. This latter type of pattern, though distressing to children, may be less profound in its impact than family patterns exhibiting a long-lasting power struggle.

Not all children, however, are similarly affected by a particular marital pattern and the disruption of the family through divorce. Age and sex affect the child's perceptions of and participation in family process. These differences will also be shown.

Finally, the child's experience is affected by the quality of the parent/child relationship. In some family patterns, marital conflict is contained between parents, and the child/parent relationship suffers less disruption. If a child is able to retain a warm relationship with at least one parent, he or she suffers fewer negative consequences during the period of separation and divorce.

Destructive Family Patterns. Clinical researchers have described two types of marital patterns in divorcing families that have a distressing impact on children. Harris (1972) described families in the first pattern as characterized by combat, struggles for control, and undisguised hostility. He claims the children in these homes serve as "hostages." They are drawn into the marital battle and used in a variety of ways. In retaliation for the deprivation of spousal affection, one parent may use the child as a punitive weapon to deprive the other parent of affection. Or the parent may try to use the child to maintain a continuing relationship with the spouse who wishes to end the relationship. Harris stated that the child may also be seduced into a coalition demanding total allegiance with one parent and rejection of the second parent. He argued that the child in any of these hostage conditions is affected negatively; he may passively submit to the hostage condition, act out and become aggressive and hostile, or learn to manipulate his parents. Any of these processes is, of course, not constructive in the child's development.

Another research study found this same kind of marital warfare among some divorcing families. Wallerstein and Kelly (1980) describe the "embittered-chaotic" parent who draws the child into the marital battle and attempts to marshal his or her psychological support. This disturbed parent makes no attempt to shield the child from destructive hostility and conflict.

These observations from clinical research are strikingly similar to some observations made in this study. As noted in Chapter Three, the Fractured Family marital pattern, characterized by open and sometimes violent hostility, can produce hostage conditions for children. Whereas other researchers suggest that power is in some way connected to this conflict—for example, that marital partners are engaged in continuing struggles for domination (Harris) or that one parent feels victimized by the divorce (Wallerstein and Kelly)—I have connected power more directly to the marital and parenting style. In this study, families with a large imbalance in power between husband and wife created hostage conditions for children. The husband's excessive power combined with the wife's frustrated dependency to create a volatile setting for a power struggle, in which one or both partners used all resources at their disposal, including the children. Conversely, hostage conditions were not found in marriages in which power between husband and wife was more balanced. Perfect Model marriages, for example, did not produce such desperate power struggles, in which the child became a pawn. I would argue, therefore, that excessive power and domination, such as abuse, by one partner within a marriage leads not only to distress in the other spouse but to profoundly disturbing conditions for the children. Abuse from the more powerful parent flows into and colors the child's experience, just as the helpless rage projected by the dependent spouse immobilizes the child and contributes to feelings of helplessness and anxiety.

In such a home, divorce, if it really means the end of a destructive pattern, may be a relief to the child. Unfortunately, these patterns normally have a long history and may continue even after divorce. Physical separation of the family into two households may serve simply to intensify and make more visible the child's role as hostage or pawn, torn between two conflicting households.

A second type of pattern also has destructive consequences for the child, but the impact seems to be more short-term. Several researchers have noted that in some families one parent may become the victim and may attempt to elicit a supporting response from the child. Beal (1979), Weiss (1979a), and Steinzor (1969) describe these situations of role reversal. However, they all suggest that these role reversals are temporary and are discontinued as both the parent and child become aware of this incongruity.

In several families in this study, a similar pattern of role reversal occurred as the child assumed the role of caretaker. In these families, however, this reversal between parent and child was preceded by a power reversal within the marriage. Characteristically, the woman gained power as she moved beyond the home to a career or new relationship outside the marriage. Her growth occurred at a time when the man was losing ground in his career struggle and was either unemployed or dissatisfied with his progress. Unlike the Fractured Families, these families were not characterized by a severe imbalance in power accumulated over a long period of time. Rather, a shift occurred toward the end of the marriage. Emotional responses, though intense, were contained within a brief period of time. There is some reason to believe that this type of marital pattern has a less devastating impact on the child. Emotional reactions are specifically related to a particular situation, which appears more temporary in nature. Perhaps as the victimized parent regains control of his or her life, the parent/child relationship may be restored and placed in proper perspective.

Age, Sex, and Vulnerability of the Child. Not all children are similarly affected by a particular style of family interaction. Even within the same home, boys and girls of different ages may respond differently. Of all ages and sex groups, boys in their latency period (ages six to ten) appear to be most vulnerable to family disruption. Several researchers and clinicians have discussed the "conduct problems" these boys tend to exhibit following family separation. Although observers use similar language to describe these aggressive, rebellious behaviors, they do not agree on the reasons for this particular pattern of behavior.

Wallerstein and Kelly (1980) found that boys in the latency period suffered greatly during the separation period. Their father's absence threatened their world, and they became quite anxious. Regardless of the father's degree of warmth and closeness to the boys before divorce, these boys felt a keen sense of loss. Using a developmental approach, Wallerstein and Kelly stated that boys at this age tried to remain loyal to both parents and at times this double loyalty was psychologically costly to them. They did not have the defenses of older children or the ability to express their own anger, particularly with their fathers. They did, however, express their anger with their mothers. Wallerstein and Kelly also found that if the father was abusive toward the mother, these young boys imitated this abusive behavior.

Psychoanalytic literature also describes behavioral problems boys exhibit when they live with their mothers. In his review on children at risk from divorce, Anthony (1974) noted this tendency of boys to behave like their fathers and explained that an unconscious collusion exists between son and remaining parent (mother) to re-create the absent father. The mother manipulates the child into playing the part of the father, and thus the wife/husband struggle is carried on through the mother/son relationship (Anthony, 1974, p. 471). McDermott (1970) suggests a similar interpretation when he describes how the child assumes in the mother's eyes certain characteristics of the father. Anthony and McDermott perceive the child's behavior as a response to the mother's unconscious encouragement rather than as a direct imitation of the father's behavior. Their failure to examine the father's participation in child rearing results in an assignment of responsibility to the mother only. They thus assume the same kind of cultural bias reflected by the stereotypes discussed earlier in this chapter.

Tooley (1976) also describes a similar behavioral pattern but has still another interpretation. She associates the boy's aggressive behavior with his attempts to create a more stable home structure by becoming the "man of the house." Her clinical data indicate these young boys frequently showed antisocial, rebellious, unmanageable behavior. She believes this "powerful behavior" emerged as these young boys perceived their world was threatened. Their fathers left home, and their mothers had difficulty coping with the myriad financial problems. Women who had not worked had difficulty finding a job that paid enough to support the family. The son, exposed to fearful insecurity and the vulnerability of his mother's position, took on the father's role as he perceived his father would play it. He imposed a harsh order on his younger siblings and aggressively accosted the outside world. Tooley maintains that increasing the women's ability to assert themselves both within and outside the home allows these young boys to relax and relinquish the protective role.

Both Weiss and McDermott agree with Tooley that the single-parent household does place an extra burden on children. While older children may respond to added responsibilities by becoming more independent and mature, younger children may be overwhelmed by these demands (Weiss, 1979a).

Beal (1979), in his comments on this friction between mother and son, has still another explanation. He explains that the custodial parent, usually the mother, is often held as more responsible for divorce because she is more responsive to the children. The child perceives that most of what happens to him in the family is determined more by the mother than by the father. Her accessibility, closeness, and responsiveness make her appear the more responsible parent, and he directs his anger toward her.

In this study I found similar situations in which boys aged six to ten exhibited aggressive, unmanageable behavior during the separation period. Like children described by other researchers, these boys directed their anger toward their mothers, but they also exhibited another behavior parallel to and alternating with the aggressive outbursts—a protective, loving behavior. They were very protective of their mothers and showed some concern for their safety and vulnerability. For example, one boy had to check and double-check the windows and doors every night at his mother's house to be sure they were locked. When he was not with her, he worried about her safety.

Boys with these conduct problems were located in homes in which the father was fairly aggressive and the mother appeared quite vulnerable. I interpreted alternating aggressive and protective behaviors as related to the child's split between two parents. In their aggressive behaviors, these young male children identified with and imitated their fathers; but they were also drawn by affection to their mothers. They tried to imitate their fathers but were then remorseful over the pain this caused for their mothers. Thus, boys of this age appear most affected by marital patterns in which men have excessive power and women have low status and little power.

Children from other families may not respond with the same kind of aggressive, acting-out behavior, but that does not mean, of course, that marital stress did not have an effect on them. Anthony (1974, p. 466) reminds the reader: "Whereas the children from conflicted marriages are inclined to be irritable, restless, aggressive, and difficult, the children from devitalized marriages generally react with flatness and lack of zest. For the family as a whole, the home becomes a 'habit cage,' and continuation is ensured by the absence of any alternatives."

My data are not extensive enough to examine this proposition, but it is quite possible that while the children in the Fractured Families appeared most troubled, the children from other family patterns, such as Fragile Bond, had equally serious problems that simply were not defined as problems. Teachers and parents may be less apt to define a shy, depressed, withdrawn child as troubled but are quick to perceive the aggressive, acting-out child as disturbed. Quite possibly, different marital patterns produce different behavioral responses in children depending on their age and sex. Some marital patterns appear more devastating than others to certain populations of children, but this should not obscure the fact that marital stress of all types does produce suffering for most children. As Anthony concluded, "The quality of the marriage prior to divorce, therefore, has a close relationship to the quality of the disturbance engendered in the child. Conflicted marriages make for conflicted children, 'emotional divorce' breeds affectionless children, skewed marriages lead to dominant or dependent children, and neurotic marriages may so load the child with unconsciously transferred feelings, reactivated from liked or disliked parental siblings, that nothing the child can do in reality makes any difference to the way he is treated" (1974, p. 467).

Protecting the Child: Maintenance of the Parent/Child Bond. Although most children may experience some difficulties during the divorce period, the impact on them may be alleviated if they are able to retain a good relationship with at least one parent. In a study of children in divorcing families, Hess and Camara (1979) found that children's behaviors were strongly affected by the quality of their relationships with their parents. Those children who continued to enjoy a high-quality relationship with both parents showed less aggression, had better social relationships, and were more productive in their schoolwork. Functioning a little less effectively were those children who maintained a good relationship with only one parent. Children with poor relationships with both parents appeared the most vulnerable to the divorce experience; they had the most difficulties in all areas of social and academic life. This study demonstrates a rather striking, unusually high correlation between parent/child relationships and the children's adjustment.

Findings from this study appear consistent with Hess and Camara's findings. I did not gather data from the children, and my conclusions must, therefore, be tentative. Interview material from the parents, however, revealed some rather striking differences in children's responses to the divorce. In response to questions about the children's functioning, some parents reported their children were having many social, psychological, and academic problems, whereas other parents reported only minor difficulties in adjustment. Further analysis showed that the children with the most problems were usually located in those homes where both parents showed a low level of nurturance and efficacy. Children who had two parents, or even one, demonstrating high levels of efficacy and nurturance appeared to have fewer problems following the divorce.

Again, certain marital patterns appear to protect and encourage high-quality parent/child bonds, while other patterns appear to be destructive to parenting. The Fragile Bond pattern, for example, apparently encourages high-quality mother/child relationships, whereas the Perfect Model pattern is characterized by high-quality mother/child and father/child bonds. In Unformed Families, the child has little protection, as one parent, the mother, shows little commitment to either the marriage or the children. In these homes, the child is more dependent on the father for nurturing. If the father is similarly uncommitted to the family, the child cannot rely on any consistent relationship with either parent. Similarly, in the more stressful Fractured Families, both parents are often retreating from their parenting responsibilities, and the child suffers poor relationships with both parents.

Summary

In conclusion, divorce is not a unidimensional event, inflicting a similar negative impact on all family members. It is a highly variable event, dependent on the interweaving of many complex factors. In this chapter I have stressed the impact one factor—the politics of the marriage—has on the family. I have argued that the distribution of power between husband and wife has far-reaching consequences for the children as well as for the marital partners.

In this emphasis on power within the family, I do not wish to imply that other factors may be ignored. Finances, for example, are a very important consideration, particularly for women and children. Social and kin support systems may color the family's experience of divorce. Social and psychological support may soften the disruptive impact of the divorce, while the absence of such support intensifies the loneliness and anxiety experienced during this period.

In this study I have focused on the key elements of power, status, and love because these elements are critical to understanding the dynamics of family life and are less clearly understood than the more tangible elements of finances and kin and social support systems. Future research studies of divorcing families may be able to create a collage, which will combine and sensitively portray the interweaving of many structural and interactional factors impinging on these families in crisis.

8

Helping Parents and Children Through Crisis and Divorce

As the stories of these forty families have unfolded, three major issues have emerged: the shaping of family patterns and evolution of powering within marriage, the resolution of custodial issues, and the divorcing family's use of the legal process.

A major portion of the analysis has focused on the development of different marital and parenting patterns. Within each pattern, the husband and wife developed different styles of negotiating with each other. I have noted, however, that few couples were able to achieve equity in their relationships. More often than not, internal relationships reflected the inequitable standing of women in the larger society. Two events, in particular, affected the balance of power within marriage: the birth of the first child and the woman's employment. Although these were

169

discrete issues, they created similar kinds of problems for the couple. The arrival of children and the woman's employment created additional responsibilities and contributed to an overload. The couple had to decide how the work would be divided and who would assume responsibilities for tasks. The addition of a parenting or work role also affected self-identity. For some, identities expanded as they experienced competence and satisfaction in a new role; for others, who felt overwhelmed or unable to perform according to acceptable standards, these new roles threatened their feelings of competency. Changes in self-perception triggered changes in the partner's perceptions and in the interaction within the marriage. Additional responsibilities and changed self-images also activated struggles over priorities. New dilemmas emerged as mates disagreed about the priorities of the worker, mate, and parent roles.

The resolution of child custody was a second important area for analysis and discussion. Initially I perceived that physical custody would be the primary focus within this book. As the stories unfolded, however, I realized that the actual physical location of children with either parent may be less significant in their development than other factors within the family's life. The quality of the child's bond with each parent appeared to be of utmost importance. The ongoing relationship between mother and father also had a powerful impact on the child during this critical period. Although physical custody was an important issue for all family members, the maintenance or severing of family bonds was undoubtedly most critical to the child's feelings of security and well-being.

A third area—the family's use of the legal process—has received less attention and will be discussed in more detail in this last chapter. Many families resolved critical issues before they contacted lawyers and had minimal contact with the legal process. For other families, however, the legal process was very important. In fact, it appeared that some families expanded the family "game" and added new players as they enlisted the support of lawyers, court counselors, judges, and therapists. This process highlighted family rules and strategies, making them more visible. These families' approach to the legal process illustrated the extension of powering within the marriage to powering in the courts and community.

If these research conclusions are to serve any lasting purpose, two major questions must be answered. First, to what extent can the information gleaned from these forty families contribute to an understanding of other families? Second, how can this information be used by professionals who work with troubled families?

On the first issue of generalizing research conclusions, it must be noted that these families differed in several ways from other families in the United States. They all decided to divorce, but two out of three couples in this society do not choose this way to resolve marital problems. They also lived in an urban area in California, long known for its nontraditional approaches to family life. Finally, the men were all employed as white-collar workers or professionals. To what extent can the experiences of the people in this book shed any light on the experiences of other couples who remain married, who live in different parts of the country, or who belong to a different class? In this chapter a review of research by other social scientists may clarify the extent to which the marital and parenting experiences of these forty families are similar to or different from the experiences of families in a larger population.

In response to the second question of application of research findings, I believe that the value of research must ultimately rest in the application of that knowledge to life situations. Research findings that remain obscure and known only to a select group of family sociologists have limited utility. The ultimate goal of this research project has been to generate information that can be used to improve the quality of life for men, women, and children within the family unit.

This chapter extends the conclusions in this book through a discussion of relevant material contributed by the social scientists. It also suggests ways in which this information can be used by professionals for more effective intervention with troubled families. Discussion centers on three different areas or points within the family's history when professionals may effectively intervene to assist the family. The first is at those major turning points within the family's development, such as the period following the birth of the first child or the wife's changes in employment. At these points a creative therapist may help families avoid frustrating impasses and formulate effective, healthy patterns.

The second point of intervention may occur as the family approaches separation. Lawyers and therapists are sometimes called on to help the divorcing family resolve questions of physical custody of the children. Finally, some divorcing families use the legal system quite extensively. Lawyers, judges, court counselors, mental health professionals must then help the family assess the child's best interests, balance his or her interests with the parent's rights, and guide the family through the legal process.

In a discussion of these interventions, I acknowledge two personal biases. First, I believe that marriage cannot be played as a zero-sum, or no-win, game, nor should it be manipulated to benefit one partner and exploit the other. To be satisfying and productive, marriage must offer some benefits to both partners. Efforts to advance the interests of one party at the expense of the other often have a negative impact on both parties. Even in a contested custody battle, an adversarial position often results in an empty victory, as both parties deplete their personal resources and endure personal suffering.

Second, I assume a systemic rather than an individualistic orientation. I view the family as an interactive unit and perceive the resolution of problems through that perspective. It is this family unit that must be treated, not isolated individuals who are identified as "problems" within it. Effective changes must occur within the entire unit; they cannot be limited to changes in one or two individuals.

Equity Within the Home

Research on these forty families illustrated the powerful impact of two events on the marriages. As indicated earlier, the arrival of the first child and the woman's employment often activated a power struggle as men and women confronted issues of work overload, changes in self-identity, and rearranged priorities in work and family roles.

Transition to Parenthood. In a review of literature on child rearing, Pohlman stated, "The decade that follows a woman's first pregnancy is often a dreary, lonely, frustrating one. ... The heavy psychological costs women experience during this period cannot but affect their husbands, their marriage relationships, and the parents' relations with their children" (1969, p. 153).

Sociologists who have studied the period immediately following childbirth vary in the extent to which they agree with Pohlman. Two of the first studies, by LeMasters (1957) and Dyer (1963), found couples who experienced this period as a severe or extensive crisis. Later studies, however, found only moderate or slight crisis reported by young parents of newborns (Hobbs, 1965; Hobbs and Cole, 1976; Russell, 1974). Some have objected to the rather negative term *crisis* and have designated this as a "transition period" (Hobbs, 1965; Rossi, 1968). Whether the adjustment is measured as "moderate" or "severe" and whether it is labeled as "crisis" or "transition," however, there is little doubt that this is a major period of adjustment for young couples. In a review of research in the seventies, Spanier and Lewis (1980) concluded that the birth of the first child had a negative impact on marriage.

The profound impact of the first child on the marriage has been documented further by another series of studies on the family life cycle. These studies have generally shown that marital satisfaction is highest during the first few years of married life, then drops sharply at the birth of the first child and remains at a similar level during the preschool, school-age, and teenage years (Blood and Wolfe, 1960; Burr, 1970; Glenn and Weaver, 1978; Miller, 1976; Rollins and Cannon, 1974; Rollins and Feldman, 1970).

Although Rollins and Cannon (1974) found no significant differences between men's and women's responses to the various stages of the life cycle, most researchers have found that women's feelings of happiness and satisfaction with marriage are more affected by the presence of children than men's (Bort-

ner, Bohn, and Hultsch, 1974; Burr, 1970; Glenn and McLanahan, 1982; Renee, 1970; Rollins and Feldman, 1970). In a recent longitudinal study that followed couples from the pregnancy through the eighth month after the baby was born,
Miller and Sollie (1980) found that although both men and
women reported greater personal stress, only women indicated
more marital stress. Waldron and Routh (1981) also found that
women reported less satisfaction with their marriage after the
baby was born, but the men's scores did not change. From their
review of the literature, Spanier and Lewis (1980) concluded
that mothers have a more difficult time adjusting to the infant
than fathers do.

These reports corroborate the experiences of many wom-
en in this study, who reported increased stress after the birth of
the first child and less marital satisfaction. There are obviously
wide variations in both the intensity of couples' reactions to the
birth of a child and the degree to which this event has a temporary or more permanent effect, but little is known at this time
about the situational conditions mediating the impact of the
first child (Spanier and Lewis, 1980).

Family Responses to Women's Employment. Early research in marital relationships used resource theory to hypothe-
size a shift in responsibilities occurring as the wife entered the
labor force. Blood and Wolfe (1960) argued that as the wife became overloaded, the husband assumed more responsibility for
housework. As she ran out of time, he gave more time to the
family. This argument appeals to one's sense of the family as a
balancing system that adjusts itself internally in response to
pressures from within and outside the system. It projects a desirable image of equity—as one partner brings more beneficial resources into the home, the other partner is willing to expend
more of his or her resources. Interpretations of their research
findings supported these assumptions. Blood and Wolfe found
that as women entered employment, their husbands undertook
a greater number of tasks within the home. Similarly, Young and
Willmott (1974) found in a British study that as women worked
longer hours outside the home, men contributed more in the
home. They argued that women's employment led to a desegre-
gation of roles within the home and a "symmetrical family."

Time studies in the 1970s, however, cast doubt on this argument and showed a lack of equity in exchange—husbands did not assume more responsibility for work when their wives were employed. In a stratified random sample of 1,296 households, Walker and Woods (1976) found that men worked 1.6 hours a day in the house, regardless of whether their wives were employed. Their participation in household tasks did not vary with size of family or age of children. Two exceptions to this occurred when the family included a child under the age of one or more than five children. With a baby and an employed wife, husbands increased their work in the home from 1.6 to 2.9 hours per day. With more than five children in the home and employed wives, men contributed 2.4 hours to housework. Neither of these increases was large; the latter involved an .8-hour increase, or an additional 48 minutes of work daily for men with more than five children.

In contrast, women's hours in housework varied greatly, depending on employment, family size, and age of children. When women returned to work, they dropped their hours in housework from an average of 8.1 hours per day to 4.8 hours. Employed women with over five children put in 6.3 hours per day of housework, compared with their husbands' 2.4 hours per day. Employed women with children under one spent 7.5 hours in housework, compared with the husbands' 2.9 hours.

Walker and Woods interviewed and obtained time records from wives only; data may, therefore, underestimate the husband's contributions to the household. Meissner, Humphreys, Meis, and Scheu (1975) conducted a time study with 340 couples and interviewed the men and women separately. Their results were similar: husbands' participation in housework did not increase with their wives' employment. Husbands spent about four to five hours a week in housework, regardless of whether their wives were housewives or employed part-time, full-time, or overtime. With extended employment, women's total workload increased from about forty-six hours a week (housewives) to seventy hours per week (working overtime plus housework), but as these women's workload increased, their husbands' total workload in job and housework actually declined from about 58 hours a week to 55. Like the Walker and Woods study, this study also found that children added to the wives' overload but added little to the men's housework or total workload.

Interview and survey studies of dual-work families have supported these time studies and have added some insights into the meaning of this overload for families. Berkove (1979), Holmstrom (1972), Paloma and Garland (1971), Rapoport and Rapoport (1976), and Yogev (1981) all found a disparity between ideals and actual behavior. In particular, dual-career couples with college educations and professional careers espoused a commitment to egalitarian ideals but practiced a traditional division of labor within the home. The wife, in most cases, made the necessary adjustments to overload and strain of overload (Paloma and Garland, 1971).

In a study of reentry women students, Hooper (1979) illustrated how divisive this issue of task responsibility can be for couples. She found that of the twenty-four couples, only six could be classified as "egalitarian." That is, the husbands, often along with the children, assumed greater responsibilities as their wives returned to school. They were also emotionally supportive of their wives' ambitions and goals. In another six households, called "labor by agreement," the women retained the same responsibilities as before. In these homes it appeared the family had tacitly agreed that the woman's return to school would not disturb the other family members. She herself expected to maintain the same responsibilities in the home and felt she could not impose on other family members for help. These families remained content as husbands enjoyed the positive growth in their wives and women were stimulated by their new areas of endeavor. In half the homes (twelve), arrangements were not satisfactory and resulted in conflict. In these homes, classified as "labor by disagreement," the wives tried to enlist more help, but husbands resisted, often with anger. Children in these families were also less supportive of the mother's activities. In summary, in half the families in this study, the families were obviously involved in a struggle over roles and tasks, and in only one quarter did the couples agree on rearranging responsibilities.

In an analysis of two national surveys, Staines, Pleck,

Shepard, and O'Connor (1978) found that role load had a deleterious effect on women's attitudes toward their marriage. Women with the greatest overload—employed wives with preschoolers who reported often "feeling rushed" and who wanted more help from husbands—more frequently indicated they had thought about divorce or wished they had married someone else.

These studies indicate that wives' employment can provoke tensions within the family. The number of families who are able to resolve these issues equitably is probably still a minority. As Rapoport and Rapoport (1976) conclude, this issue may take another generation to solve.

Identity changes associated with work roles are not as easy to measure as distribution of labor within the home. In a review of research on the impact of employment on mothers, Nye (1974) concluded that employed mothers had a more positive self-image than housewives. Burke and Weir (1976) indicated employed wives reported better mental and physical health than housewives.

Rapoport and Rapoport (1976) also report that couples seem to have some vulnerable points or "identity tension lines," at which one partner will become uncomfortable and refuse to go further. The spouse may then retreat and not force confrontation. In this way, women may minimize identity changes. They find ways to conceal their own growth and competence and allow men to retain authority in the home. In a way, these are face-saving gestures that enable men to retain cherished images of themselves. Yogev (1981) also suggests that women willingly assume more than an equal share of household work because to ask for equity in this area would be to go "too far." An identity tension line serves as a boundary on how much a wife can demand from her husband.

Work does not, of course, always have a positive impact on women's feelings of self-worth. Many studies have focused on dual-career couples and professional women. Only recently has more attention been given to dual-work families, in which the wife perceives her work as a job rather than a career. Staines and others (1978) found that education made a difference in women's responses to combined worker/family roles. Employed women with less than a high school education were less satisfied with their marriages and more often said they had thought about divorce or wished they had married someone else. Work outside the home apparently did not contribute to their personal growth or their satisfaction with the marriage. Women who work as menial laborers outside the home may feel doubly exploited at home and on the job (Rapoport and Rapoport, 1976). An unskilled, low-paid job and an overload at home certainly do not add up to liberation for these women.

Recent studies have also given more attention to the husband and have examined the impact of his wife's employment on his well-being. Evidence from these studies is conflicting. Burke and Weir (1976), for example, found that men married to working wives had poorer mental and physical health than men married to housewives. They more frequently described themselves as worrying and in lower spirits than did the husbands of housewives. They reported less satisfaction with their marriages and, interestingly enough, perceived that when disagreements arose, they were more likely resolved by a mutual give-and-take rather than by either person giving in. This finding corroborates observations made in this study. When women returned to work, the men in this study often reported they could no longer just assume their wives would follow along with their plans. They lost some of the control they once had. Perhaps this change is disconcerting and leads to some feelings of confusion and ambivalence about the marriage.

Other studies have had different outcomes. Staines and others (1978) found that men's attitudes about their marriage were not affected by the wives' employment. An interview study by Booth (1979) in Canada found very few differences between men married to housewives and men married to working wives. Differences, when found, favored the men with working wives. Dual-career studies have also found that men are positively affected by their wives' careers. Rapoport and Rapoport (1976) reported that men enjoyed their wives' personal growth and sometimes found vicarious satisfaction and excitement in their wives' careers.

In several ways, these studies support the conclusions derived from this study of forty families. Numerous time studies, interview studies, and survey studies conclude: When a woman is employed, the workload within the home is increased. Tasks are not necessarily reorganized, and the wife bears the brunt of the overload. Husbands often give verbal support to the woman's development outside the home, but in practice they assume that her employment will not involve any major changes in household routines. Women may tacitly agree and may continue to believe they can hold two jobs, with only a minimum amount of "help" from husbands and other family members. Eventually, however, this overload contributes to a resentment that undermines positive feelings about the marriage. Expressed resentment, however, may stimulate a hostile response from the husband and may not result in any change. Certain conditions may contribute to more positive outcomes for the family. When the husband perceives this employment as beneficial and when he contributes emotional and behavioral support, or when women find ways to successfully juggle responsibilities with perhaps some hired help, the wife's employment can result in benefits to all family members.

Interventions with Families. Effective intervention at critical points in the family's life may help the family create new approaches to integrating work and parenting roles. Families who fail to reach a positive resolution may separate or may continue to live together for years, but with much resentment and hostility. Scanzoni (1979) has suggested a variety of approaches to help couples create positive solutions. One, which he terms "prosocial" or "altruistic," argues that men should be encouraged to change because it is fair, just, and moral for them to change. Their changes will benefit women, children, and society in general. Some men may respond to an appeal to their altruistic concerns. They may sincerely wish to be reasonable and fair with those they love. These husbands will realize that their wives will be happier if they have opportunities to exercise options in their lives; limiting these options by direct or indirect pressures will create stress and may ultimately poison the marital life.

If men feel they will lose much by a rearrangement of their family life, they may not respond to an altruistic plea. They need to see how these changes will affect them personally. Scanzoni's second approach is based on self-interest. Men have much to gain by becoming more involved with their infants. They also benefit from their wives' careers and development outside the home. One obvious benefit is money. Men are relieved of the full responsibility of providing for the family. Dual-career studies have reported other benefits that emerge as couples creatively integrate certain job characteristics. For example, men in stable positions found their wives' involvement in entrepreneurial pursuits added some excitement to their family life. Conversely, men in occupations involving great risks found their wives' steady employment added stability and security to the family. Men in their middle years, caught in an occupational role that had gone stale over time, welcomed an opportunity to start a new venture. Their wives' steady employment made these changes possible.

Some husbands also experienced some vicarious satisfactions with their wives' careers. Rapoport and Rapoport (1976) describe couples in which the wife's job satisfied some yearning the man had. For example, the wife's career in art or writing contributed to the husband's continued interest in this area.

Some couples also derived satisfaction from resolving dilemmas of integrating work and family roles. Working out these roles was a creative process and, in itself, was gratifying (Rapoport and Rapoport, 1976).

Undoubtedly men do not foresee all these benefits when they first anticipate integrating work and parenting roles. These insights come with experience (Berkove, 1979; Spitze and Waite, 1981). A family therapist working with a couple may be able to reduce the husband's fears of loss and point out the potential for positive benefits. As they realize these benefits, men may be more willing to relinquish privileges and may, in fact, be quite relieved to give up their center-stage role.

Not all men, of course, will see it this way. Studies continue to show that conflict seems to be the rule rather than the exception. Young and Willmott (1974) argue that as society moves toward more symmetry within the family, couples will experience some transitional unhappiness, and strains will be inescapable. When there is disagreement, couples can be taught to negotiate. In this study, some families were quite inflexible and unable to negotiate. Stalemate Marriages, for example, adopted a fairly rigid pattern, as did Fractured Families. Perfect Model families, however, appeared to be more flexible and more open to negotiation.

Scanzoni (1979) stresses the importance of creativity in this process. As the couple confront new situations, they must create novel solutions. They may have no role models to imitate, but even if they do, their own particular family demands and interests may require a unique approach. These families, in particular, need therapists who are not rigid in their conceptualization of family life. If therapists can help couples avoid frustrating impasses and negotiate arrangements suitable to their needs, they will contribute much to the marriage and to the children's development within the family.

It is important in these negotiations that the couple work for a "maximum joint profit" rather than "maximum individual profit" (Scanzoni, 1979). If one or both partners negotiate for their own benefit, the results may be only minimally satisfying.

The most effective approach to this dilemma of achieving equity within the home may be to perceive liberation in a broad sense. It is not just women who are being "liberated" from oppressive roles, but men as well. An extensive literature has emerged that points out the need for men to consider the positive benefits they may experience through change (Farrell, 1974; Fasteau, 1974; David and Brannon, 1976; Pleck and Sawyer, 1974). Hooper (1979) points out that programs that attempt to help the woman change personal behaviors will be much more effective if they treat the family as a unit rather than offer assistance to the wife only. When a couple are able to see that some changes will result in greater rewards for both and a more mutually satisfying relationship, they may respond, even though those changes are not easy to make.

However, if men and women hang onto a conflict perspective that assumes the more women gain, the more men lose, it is understandable that men will resist change. When approached in this way, the marriage results in a stalemate with frustration for both partners.

An effective approach requires that partners give up their individual, competitive positions and adopt a more family-oriented, cooperative view. In a society based on individual competition and achievement, this change is not easy to achieve and may involve much struggle and pain. That may be the price men and women have to pay to create homes that provide healthy, nurturing environments for all members within the family.

Effectiveness of Nontraditional Custodial Arrangements

The second major focus in this book has been the child within the separating family. How can the family resolve questions of physical custody in ways that are beneficial to the children? As laws and social attitudes have changed in recent years, the entire process of determining custody has become more ambiguous. Some commentators have feared that indeterminate standards will lead to more traumatic custody battles, which are socially, emotionally, and financially costly to all participants. To avoid these high social costs, Ellsworth and Levy (1969, p. 203) argued that regardless of the statutory standard, since men in any particular case may be "only marginally better than the mother or even much worse," they should be discouraged from trying to get custody of their children. Steinzor also argued that women should continue to receive custody of their children because they have been socialized into the parenting role. He noted that men are not clamoring for custody (Steinzor, 1969, pp. 70-72).

These views were expressed more than a decade ago, but undoubtedly many professionals today have some misgivings about nontraditional arrangements. For example, a guidebook published by the Family Law Committee of the Minnesota State Bar Association recommended fathers should not have custody except in rare cases. This report contended fathers were unqualified psychologically and emotionally and would not have time to supervise and care for their children (Mendes, 1979).

This point of view raises several questions. Can men balance their work responsibilities with child care? Can a father meet his children's needs, particularly their emotional needs? How effective will a father be with his daughter, particularly as she approaches puberty and adolescence?

Joint or shared custody has become increasingly popular in recent years, but how does it really work? Can couples who could not agree in marriage agree about sharing their children after the divorce?

Questions and objections raised about these nontraditional custodial arrangements are not trivial. Why should the courts abolish maternal preference and permit consideration of alternatives that may, after all, not work as well as traditional arrangements? If father custody and joint custody are less desirable and workable than mother custody, the high emotional and financial costs of attempting to resolve these contested cases cannot be justified. The issue that must be addressed is: How effective are the nontraditional custodial arrangements? Is there any evidence from behavioral science that permits a knowledgeable comparison of these different custodial arrangements?

Father Custody. Very few studies have systematically compared the different custody conditions. Most studies have instead focused on one type of arrangement. One study systematically compared father-custody arrangements with mother-custody families. DeFrain and Eirick (1981) compared responses from thirty-three divorced single-parent fathers and thirty-eight divorced single-parent mothers in Nebraska. They found that only one of sixty-three items statistically differentiated between these two groups: the parent's willingness to encourage children to take sides between spouses. Nearly a third of the fathers said they encouraged children to take sides, while only one mother did so. On all other measures of child rearing, relations with ex-spouses, and feelings about single parenting, mothers and fathers were quite similar.

In an interview study of mothers and fathers with custody, Ambert (1982) found differences in the children's responses to parents based on sex of custodial parent and socioeconomic status. Custodial fathers reported better child behavior toward

them and said their children often expressed appreciation for
the father's efforts in parenting. Children of custodial mothers
seldom expressed this appreciation, and the behavior of children
toward mothers in low-income families was by far more difficult than children's behavior in higher-income mother-custody
homes. This study, though based on only twenty-seven cases, is
provocative because it suggests intimate interactions between
child behavior, parental adjustment, and economic status. Children may assume women are supposed to take care of them and
there is no need to appreciate women who do the expected. Fathers who assume these responsibilities are rare, and both the
children and father may perceive that the children should be
grateful to him, just as coworkers and friends admire him (Ambert, 1982, p. 82). In lower-income families, the children may
also resent the deprivations and may hold women responsible
for them. Since men generally receive higher wages than women
in this society, father-custody families may be less apt to suffer
changes in income as they move from married to single status
(Little, 1982).

Both these studies suggest that children are responsive to
social norms that establish the mother as the primary parent.
They assume the mother will continue caring for them. They
may feel quite critical of the mother who leaves and appreciate
the father who stays.

Several other studies have not been comparative but have
focused entirely on fathers with custody and have described the
father's adjustment to this new role and his ability to care for
the children's needs. They have consistently reported that men
have little difficulty in assuming responsibility for maintenance
of the home and household tasks (Gasser and Taylor, 1976;
Mendes, 1976; Orthner, Brown, and Ferguson, 1976; Smith and
Smith, 1981). They have also found that fathers are able to syn-
chronize their occupational and familial responsibilities (Mendes, 1976; Smith and Smith, 1981). Some fathers changed jobs;
others reduced workloads after they received custody of their
children. Others used community services and were able to continue their same work commitments.

A second important finding emerging from these studies

was the father's ability and willingness to spend time in the fathering role; single-parent fathers did not simply turn over their responsibilities to a mother substitute (Orthner and Lewis, 1979). They relied primarily on group child care facilities for the care of young children during work hours and assumed primary responsibility for children in the evenings and on weekends. Older children cared for themselves after school. Like single mothers, these men helped children structure their free time after school through arranged activities and sports; they provided indirect supervision through extensive use of the telephone (Mendes, 1976).

It appears that the tendency in single-parent families, whether headed by males or females, is for parents to maintain a primary parenting role but to also expect children to regulate their own behaviors and to participate more in household responsibilities. These parental demands may contribute to the child's development of self-reliance, independence, and maturity (Orthner, Brown, and Ferguson, 1976; Weiss, 1979a). Thus, responsibility for self and a reallocation of work and responsibility within the home may be a consequence of the restructuring of the household from two parents to one parent and may not be related to the sex of the custodial parent.

A third finding addresses the issue of father/daughter relationships: fathers may be able and willing to supervise their children, but are they as effective with their daughters as with their sons? In a study of boys and girls from father-custody, mother-custody, and intact homes, Santrock and Warshak (1979) found very few differences associated with family structure alone: The more significant differences occurred in the combined factors of custodial condition and sex of child. Boys in father-custody families were more mature and socially competent and had higher self-esteem than boys in mother-custody families; conversely, girls in mother-custody homes were less demanding and more mature and independent than girls in father-custody families.

In the interview studies, fathers expressed little anxiety about raising girls. They did acknowledge some difficulties with specific issues of dress, appearance, and sex education (Mendes,

1976) and sought help for their daughters from female friends, teachers, neighbors, and physicians.

Research studies on father custody have all used small, nonrepresentative samples. They therefore raise some questions about validity and generalizability. The findings, however, are impressive because they are so consistent. Research studies including men from all socioeconomic groups in diverse geographical locations have found that fathers are able to manage parenting responsibilities and combine them with their work. These fathers often realized some side benefits in their new role: "These fathers feel quite capable and successful in their ability to be the primary parent of their children. The confidence they express and the satisfaction they seem to derive in fatherhood is very difficult to deny. We had anticipated a significant problem with role strain and adjustment to being the primary parent but we found little evidence that this is a major handicap. All of the fathers experienced some problems but these were not unlike the difficulties experienced in most families. The sense of pride in being able to cope with the challenge of parenthood and seeing their children mature under their guidance is a major compensating force" (Orthner, Brown, and Ferguson, 1976, p. 436).

Being a single parent is not, of course, an easy task. George and Wilding (1972) discuss the financial problems that plagued the fathers in their British study. These men experienced a real financial strain that continued for one to six years after the wife's departure. Single fathers also experience some loneliness and depression as they face parenting responsibilities without a mate (George and Wilding, 1972; Katz, 1979).

The single-parent role entails heavy responsibilities and can be burdensome. Like women, men do not all respond similarly to the burdens and pleasures of this role. One researcher linked the father's effectiveness in this role with the trajectory he and his family followed to the condition of father custody. O'Brien (1981) found three types of trajectories followed by men with custody of their children. The Conciliatory Negotiators arrived at an amicable agreement with their wives about custody. In both demographic characteristics and family process, these families were remarkably similar to the families in the Shared Parenting group in this study (see Chapter Six). Both parents were well educated and employed in professional and managerial occupations; few women were housewives. Furthermore, these marriages were apparently more egalitarian than other marriages, and men had participated more in child rearing and household work before the divorce. As the separation approached, these couples were able to negotiate arrangements that appeared favorable for their children as well as for themselves. These families apparently experienced less difficulty during the separation period as the mothers retained contact with their children and the fathers expressed both confidence and pleasure in their role as primary parent (O'Brien, 1981, pp. 185-187).

O'Brien's second group, the Hostile Seekers, were quite comparable to Fractured Families in this study, who were less committed to the parenting role. These men were unable to separate their children's welfare from their own marital conflicts and hostilities. They sought to obtain revenge and punish their wives for undesirable behavior, particularly for adultery. Some also apparently hoped that retaining the children would eventually entice women back into the home. These men had been less involved with child rearing before the divorce and appeared more anxious and insecure in their parenting role after the divorce.

O'Brien's third group, the Passive Acceptors, appeared most similar to the Unformed Families in this study. This group included more socially deprived men and women; most of the men were in skilled and semiskilled occupations. Women had few financial resources and frequently had to rely on kin for support. Many of these women apparently left their families quite abruptly and failed to maintain contact with their children or ex-spouses after the separation. Although these husbands tended to have more experience with their children before divorce than other men, they were not as confident in their roles as parents. They expressed considerable conflict and tended to overemphasize the mother's role. Apparently they felt limited in the degree to which they could provide for their children.

These studies and my study of forty families indicate that fathers with custody cannot be typecast. In fact, in comparing male and female single parents, there may be more variation *within* groups than *between* groups. That is, within each group of fathers and mothers with custody, there are wide differences in approaches to parenting and acceptance of the single parenting role. Between groups there may be many similarities as parents, male or female, respond to similar kinds of conditions. Response to the single parenting role may be predicated more on the conditions surrounding this role than on sex of parent. Thus, parents, male or female, who *choose* this role and enjoy the support of the ex-spouse find their role as single parents much easier. Children are more relaxed and easier to handle, and the parent's effectiveness is supported rather than undermined. Men and women who are propelled into single parenting by the mate's desertion suffer severe adjustment problems. Adjusting to an overload of parenting responsibility and the trauma of rejection by a mate contributes to less effective parenting, at least temporarily.

The long-term adjustment of both mothers and fathers with custody of their children and the effects on their children cannot be predicted, as no longitudinal studies of families with different trajectories in divorce have been completed. What little evidence there is suggests that either parent, male or female, can perform very adequately as a single parent, provided he or she desires to make that commitment to children and receives some support from the ex-spouse and a social network of friends and kin.

Joint Custody. During the past decade a new form of custody has emerged among divorcing families: joint or shared custody. Although joint custody has only recently gained attention in the courtrooms, it has probably existed for many years. Varieties of shared custody have probably been worked out by couples who wish to share responsibilities for their children but do not seek approval for these arrangements from the court (Folberg and Graham, 1979).

Shared custody is in many ways an ideal arrangement; it avoids overburdening one parent with primary care and allows both parents day-to-day contact with and responsibility for the child. Continuing involvement with both parents is a key factor in the child's satisfactory adjustment to the divorce situation (Anthony, 1974; Wallerstein and Kelly, 1980).

Although this form of sharing responsibility may seem an ideal solution for both the child and parents, the notion of joint custody has aroused a great deal of opposition. Most of this dissent has come from lawyers and judges. Miller (1979), an advocate of joint custody, summarizes arguments that have been made against it: (1) Joint custody creates an unstable, impermanent condition for children and does not assure them of permanent, long-term placement. (2) It doesn't work—parents who divorce are not able to cooperate and work out a shared arrangement with their children. (3) Having two homes is confusing for children. They encounter two different life-styles and value systems and may have difficulty coping with these different styles. Two homes may very well add up to no home (Roberts and Roberts, 1974). (4) Joint custody creates practical problems. This form of custody requires more money for two homes and two sets of everything. It also involves some logistical problems in transportation and scheduling. (5) Finally, joint custody is really an evasive action undertaken by parents and the legal system. It may provide an easy way out for parents who do not want to hurt one partner's feelings. If the mother is "unfit," she can save face by agreeing to joint custody rather than give up custody to the father. Joint custody is an easy way out for the legal system because it doesn't have to "predict the future" (Miller, 1979).

Bodenheimer (1977) notes another problem with joint custody—interstate adjudication. If one parent moves to another state and takes the child, it will be impossible for that state to comply with the Uniform Child Custody Jurisdiction Act. This act, which has been adopted in the majority of states, gives precedence to the state in which a custody case was originally handled. If a parent attempts to move to another state and reopen custody, the second state honors the decision made by the original state and returns the case to that state. This legislation was adopted to address the issue of parental child-snatching, when parents who were dissatisfied with the resolution of custody in their own states established residence and reopened the case in another state, which they expected would act in their favor. In the interstate context, joint custody is simply undetermined custody. In that sense, Bodenheimer feels this type of arrangement simply postpones the day of reckoning when parents and courts will have to face the issue of assigning custody to one parent (Bodenheimer, 1977).

On the other side of the issue are those persons who argue that joint custody can and does work. These proponents of shared custody generally cite cases of families who have enthusiastically adopted these arrangements (Roman and Haddad, 1978). These arguments are based on personal experiences.

Empirical evidence on the advantages and problems associated with joint custody is scant. Watson (1981) found in an interview study of fathers sharing custody that these men were child-oriented and had been involved in child care during the marriage. These men reported their wives were equally involved; neither parent wanted his or her own or the mate's involvement to wane after the divorce. These couples were successful in establishing schedules that could be consistently followed. While these men emphasized the importance of cooperation in making decisions about their children, they did not view different lifestyles as a handicap to children. In fact, some felt they benefited by being exposed to two life-styles and sets of values.

Since this type of custody has received so much attention recently, research studies will undoubtedly soon appear with more definitive conclusions. Until then, professionals may have to base their recommendations on a minimal set of guidelines. The following conditions have been suggested by various proponents of joint custody: (1) Both parents must be physically and psychologically fit to care for the child. (2) Both spouses must agree to and want to continue their involvement with the child. (3) The parents must be able to cooperate in making decisions about the child. (4) It is helpful if parents live in the same geographical area and reach some agreement about mobility. They should have sufficient money for providing two homes and perhaps some overlap of clothing and toys. If not, they must be able to work out arrangements for sharing these possessions that are not burdensome and impossible for the child.

The Family and the Legal Process

Because families approach the divorce in such a variety of ways, their use of the legal system also varies. Some families, for example, have very limited contacts with lawyers and judges. They may even dispense with lawyers altogether and independently file the necessary papers. Their only contact with the courts is that moment when one of the partners presents the spousal agreement on dissolution to the judge for approval. At the other extreme, some families consult extensively with lawyers and spend many hours debating their case in the courtroom. In a prolonged custody dispute, the cast of characters can include psychologists, court-appointed social workers, neighbors, kin, and friends.

Custody battles raise numerous issues important to children and parents, as well as to the legal practitioners and mental health professionals working with these families. These issues include the following:

1. Legal and social pressures are forcing acceptance of an indeterminate, flexible standard on custody, rather than a preference for one parent. Current focus is on the "best interests of the child." What criteria can be used to determine what is best for the child?
2. Criteria for assessing the child's interests are vague and broad in scope. What procedures can be followed to gather information pertaining to the child's interests? Since the criteria include a psychological assessment, behavioral scientists may participate in the decision-making process. What role shall mental health professionals play in this process?
3. In recent years nontraditional forms of professional assistance have emerged. How can arbitration, mediation, and court investigations be used to help the family resolve its dispute?

4. The focus in child custody has shifted from the parent's rights to the child's rights, but there is little agreement about how a child can exercise his rights. Should the court appoint a lawyer to represent him? How do his rights at times conflict with the parent's rights? What procedures can be undertaken to safeguard the interests of both parents and children?

5. Vague standards and a relatively arbitrary process of decision making encourage manipulation by highly invested participants. How does politics enter into the legal process and affect determination of a case? Are there any procedures that can be undertaken to safeguard the legal process from political maneuvers?

Assessing the Child's Best Interests. A movement away from preference for one parent adds to the difficulty in determining child custody. Legal and social pressures are forcing acceptance of a more flexible, indeterminate standard, which focuses on the "best interests of the child" rather than on a traditional preference for the mother.

But what are the "best interests of the child?" How do we determine them? What criteria will be used to assess each situation? The Revised Uniform Marriage and Divorce Act provided these guidelines for determining "best interests of the child": "The court shall determine custody in accordance with the best interests of the child. The court shall consider all relevant factors including: (1) the wishes of the child's parent or parents as to his custody; (2) the wishes of the child as to his custodian; (3) the interaction and interrelationship of the child with his parent or parents, his siblings, and any other person who may significantly affect the child's best interests; (4) the child's adjustment to his home, school, and community; and (5) the mental and physical health of all individuals involved. The court shall not consider conduct of a proposed custodian that does not affect his relationship to the child" (Shepherd, 1974, pp. 172-173).

These standards are very general. Watson (1969) itemizes more specifically the types of information that are pertinent to resolution of child custody. These include assessment of school needs, material needs, need for adequate social stimulation, need for special therapy, needs relating to the quality and quantity of "parenting," need for adult models, and need for stability.

Some commentators have favored statutes providing a list of issues over those statutes offering less guidance (Benedek and Benedek, 1972; Robbins, 1974). Such a detailed list reduces the risk of overemphasis on one single factor. But Weiss points out that the judge must still consider "such elusive matters as the quality of the parent-child relationships and the nature of children's adjustment to various settings" (Weiss, 1979b, p. 330). The problem is not in the number of issues that may be specified but in the decisions required. They involve subjective assessments of the child's situation, and even the most detailed list is really little more than a "framework for subjectivity" (Weiss, 1979b, p. 330).

Role of the Mental Health Professional. Gathering information on the child is an essential but time-consuming task. Since the assessment of needs is really a psychological assessment, behavioral science experts are often included in the decision-making process. Commentators frequently assert that attorneys and judges have not received training in behavioral sciences and do not have the competence to make judgments or assess family relationships (Benedek and Benedek, 1972, 1979; Cantor and Ferguson, 1976; Fain, 1967; Inker and Perretta, 1971; Roberts and Roberts, 1974; Sheffner and Suarez, 1975; Shepherd, 1974). They further state that the legal questions may, in fact, be secondary to pathological family dynamics (Sheffner and Suarez, 1975; Roberts and Roberts, 1974). When these family issues are addressed, resolution of disputes in custody or visitation may follow. Behavioral science experts are, accordingly, exhorted to overcome any reluctance to become involved and take a definite position in the legal process (Benedek and Benedek, 1972; Sheffner and Suarez, 1975).

Other commentators are less enthusiastic about the behavioral scientist's role in adjudication of child custody. They argue that behavioral scientists' contributions are limited by inadequate psychological theory, insufficient research data, and consequently an inability to predict consequences. Okpaku (1976) argues that psychological theories are so general and vague that they cannot provide specific guidance in the resolution of difficult custody cases. In addition, psychological assumptions are virtually identical with legal presumptions that the courts have traditionally employed in awarding custody (preference for maternal care, stability of relationships); they do not provide any new information.

Okpaku, unfortunately, fails to recognize any nonpsychoanalytic theories or empirical studies. She completely ignores, for example, the vast field of child development, in which numerous studies have documented the impact of particular parenting behaviors on children. Her failure to cite even one nonpsychoanalytic study indicates her argument is limited to a critique of psychoanalytic theories and research only.

The second argument states that behavioral sciences have not produced any research evidence applicable to determination of child custody. No longitudinal studies of consequences of various forms of custody exist (Ellsworth and Levy, 1969; Okpaku, 1976). Mnookin (1975) and Okpaku (1976) further caution that the behavioral sciences, in their present state, cannot predict the consequences of various alternatives. Inadequate theory and insufficient research data make it impossible for the mental health professional to formulate recommendations for family arrangements. Mnookin also points out that the whole issue of "best interests" raises the question of values. What is "best" or most desirable in one person's perception may not necessarily be viewed by another person as "best." He poses several examples: Which is better for the child—warm relationships or discipline and self-sacrifice? Stability and security or intellectual stimulation? Even if professionals were able to predict consequences of parent/child arrangements and specific parenting behaviors, they are no better equipped than any other observer to pronounce which of these consequences is most desirable. Custody litigation is weighted down not only by a lack of real information and inability to predict but by the added burden of imposing value judgments on families, which may or may not fit with their own value systems.

What, then, is the role of the mental health professional? What information can this person add to facilitate the decision-making process? First, these professionals have a very important role in gathering information on family relationships. As skilled and trained observers, they are able to describe the actual family situation more perceptively than lawyers or other persons untrained in interpersonal behavior. A report based on these observations may be most useful to attorneys and judges. Second, such an examination is valuable if it focuses on the present rather than the future. Parent/child relationships will undoubtedly change over time, as will external conditions. No one, for example, knows how the experience of single parenting itself will change the relationship between the parent and child. It is not necessary for either the psychologist or judge to try to second-guess just what these changes will be. Third, mental health professionals are most useful in their supportive role to families. Counseling during and after the divorce alleviates stress (Kressel, Lopez-Morillas, Weinglass, and Deutsch, 1979). In fact, these professional interventions may help families make their own decisions about custody of their children, thus removing this issue from lengthy examination in the courtroom.

Finally, many legal judgments still reflect deeply instilled cultural biases. Okpaku, for example, cites agreement between legal presumptions and psychiatric assumptions. Both professions have viewed and continue to perceive the mother as the preferred parent because she is socialized into the nurturing role and is more willing to give up her career for a child (Okpaku, 1976). In her unquestioning acceptance of these premises, Okpaku fails to perceive that this is indeed the real problem: Both professions have been permeated by the same cultural biases. If behavioral science experts simply reiterate the biases already existing in the courtroom, they may add little to the proceedings. If, however, they raise questions and attempt to examine these biased assumptions, they may play a significant role. If they are able to disturb traditional thinking that is based more on fancy than on fact, they may provoke a more open examination of the child's and family's best interests.

Investigative Reports, Mediation, and Arbitration. In recent years some nonjudicial alternatives have been devised to help families resolve custody disputes. These procedures are beneficial as they remove the case from the courtroom and save valuable court time and money. In addition, they reduce the adversarial nature of the custody process. Three approaches to resolution of custody issues are the investigative report, mediation, and arbitration.

Of the three alternatives, the investigative report is most closely connected to the legal processes. Mental health professionals, usually social workers, are employed by the court to gather information on the family. They interview both parents and may interview the children if they believe it will be helpful. Since the main purpose is to gather information, the professional's contacts with the family members are primarily investigative rather than therapeutic. The professional formulates an assessment of the family situation as quickly as possible and then writes a report with recommendations for custody and visitation. Emphasis in this report is generally not on identifying one parent who may not be "fit" but on determining which parent and environment can most nearly fulfill the best interests of the child (Cantor and Ferguson, 1976). As the case proceeds through the court, the investigator must be available for cross-examination by the parents' attorneys. In making the final judgments on custody, judges tend to rely quite extensively on these reports.

The main difficulty with this approach is the limited time the investigator has to spend with each family. This professional, who is employed by the court, has an extensive caseload and has to limit the number of interviews with each family. Decisions, therefore, must be made quickly and may, at times, be based more on the intuitive insights of the therapist than on extensive information.

Mediation, a second approach to resolving custody issues, is a "process in which the parties negotiate with each other in the presence of one or more facilitators" (Gaddis, 1978, p. 43). Together with the couple, the mediator identifies issues of disagreement and emotional responses to these issues (Taylor, 1981). As the couple meets with the mediator in several sessions, they explore alternatives, make decisions, and formulate an agreement plan, which is then reviewed in the legal channels. If it is accepted by lawyers and judges, the mediator helps the family implement the plan and refers the family to community agencies if they need further assistance (Taylor, 1981).

The mediator must be a skilled and experienced professional. His or her task is not simply to act as a neutral party in gathering information (Haynes, 1980). The mediator must attempt to achieve balance between the partners; at times, this means confronting a partner who uses unfair power tactics and intervening for the less powerful person (Haynes, 1980). The mediator, therefore, must be skilled enough to identify and cope with each partner's power plays and manipulative moves. Although this process may be therapeutic for the couple, the chief objective of the professional is not to apply therapy but to help the couple negotiate a fair, workable plan. This approach is ideal as it enables couples to negotiate a plan for themselves and does not impose on them an arrangement by a third party. It does, however, require a very skilled mediator to bring about such a negotiation. Much of the success or failure of this approach may rest on the expertise of the mediator.

Arbitration, the third approach, is "the process of dispute resolution in which the parties submit the relevant information pertaining to the issues in dispute to an independent third party, who then makes the decision" (Gaddis, 1978). This approach, often used in settling labor disputes, is seldom used in family disputes. Arbitration has the advantage of using an objective third party to formulate a fair and reasonable plan, but it lacks the advantages of mediation. Couples are not involved in negotiating and resolving their problems and, consequently, may be less willing to follow the plan.

The Child's Rights in Custody Litigation. Laws have shifted their focus from parents' rights to the child's rights. At one time, children were little more than chattel to be awarded to one parent, usually the father. Custody statutes now require consideration of the child's rights, but there is little agreement about how the child will exercise her rights. Debate centers on three main issues: (1) Should the court appoint an attorney to

represent the child in the courtroom? (2) Shall the judge consider the child's preferences? If so, what weight shall be given to
these preferences, and how will this information be elicited
from the child? (3) Finally, at what points may the child's rights
conflict with the parent's rights? What procedures may the
court adopt to safeguard the interests of all parties?

The Revised Uniform Marriage and Divorce Act provides
that the court "may" appoint an attorney to represent the interests of the child (Shepherd, 1974). Advocates argue that appointing a lawyer will ensure that the parent's interests do not
supersede the child's (Hansen, 1964). They state that the court
needs independent, objective evidence that can be procured
only by a person representing the child (Hatherley, 1973; Inker
and Perretta, 1971). Lawyers representing each of the parents
cannot be expected to present information important to the
child but possibly not in their client's best interests.

Inker and Perretta (1971) argue further that children in
other types of litigation are given counsel. Juveniles in delin-
quency and adoption hearings are accorded the benefits of due
process and are represented by an attorney (Cantor and Ferguson, 1976; Hatherley, 1973). Principles of due process should,
therefore, be extended to include children in custody litigation
(Milmed, 1974).

In 1971 Wisconsin mandated the appointment of lawyers
for minor children affected by divorce. On the basis of his experience with this system, Holy (1977) advised, however, that
such representatives should not be appointed until it is clear
that custody is a real issue. In the early stages of the divorce
process, one partner may file for custody simply in response to
the emotional threat of divorce. The lawyer appointed to represent the child must give full service and not just token repre-
sentation. His or her primary responsibility is to gather information on the child's situation by interviewing the child and people who know the child (Holy, 1977; Inker and Perretta, 1971).
Since an attorney does not have special training in child development, he or she should cooperate with social workers in gathering this information.

Other commentators are not so sure appointing another

lawyer will expedite the process. Coogler (1978) argues that this will simply escalate the adversarial nature of the process. As previously discussed, the introduction of a mediator or conciliator, one who can work toward deescalation of conflict and agreement among the parties, may be more appropriate to the child's as well as the entire family's interests.

The court must also decide whether the child's preferences will be considered and what weight they shall be given. If the child's preferences are to be considered, the judge must determine procedures to elicit this information.

Custody statutes do not specify the age a child must attain before her wishes will be considered by the court. Judges have occasionally used age guidelines specified in other statutes. For example, the California Probate Code specifically allows the child over fourteen years of age to nominate her own guardian (Hatherley, 1973, p. 337). Some judges have used this age as a convenient dividing line and have given attention to the wishes of children over fourteen but have not involved children under that age (Hatherley, 1973, p. 339).

Rather than use an age guideline, courts generally try to determine whether the child has "sufficient mental capacity to make an informed and intelligent choice" (Siegel and Hurley, 1977). In reviewing the child's preferences, the courts also take into account the intensity of the child's stated wishes and possible motivations for these preferences if they appear to have been manipulated by one parent or if they reflect an alternative attractive to the child but not necessarily in his best interests (for example, the child prefers the more permissive parent or the parent who can provide more material comforts).

If a judge decides the child's wishes should be considered, he must then determine whether the child will bear witness in the open court or will speak privately with him in his chambers. A decision to call the child as witness in court is generally based on an assessment of his competency and the psychological repercussions of this experience on the child. Age, intelligence, memory, and understanding of the need for truthfulness are considered in assessing competency. The trial judge may not refuse to call the child as witness because he deems the child incompetent (Siegel and Hurley, 1977). He must call the child and examine him to determine whether he is competent. However, a judge may refuse to call the child as witness if he deems the child will suffer psychological harm from this experience.

Because witnessing in court may be a very difficult experience for the child, the judge may decide to obtain information in a private interview in chambers. This procedure protects the child from a public statement of his preferences and reduces the trauma he may experience.

The role of the child in custody litigation raises some difficult issues of due process and rights—the child's rights and the parent's rights. How may the court protect the child's rights? At what points may the exercise of her rights impinge on the parent's rights? A child has a right to express her wishes, but is she the best judge of her own "best interests"?

As previously indicated, a child may be influenced by one parent who offers some attractive advantage to the child. Although the judge may be able to identify these more obvious motivating factors, he may not have the information, training, or insight to detect other factors influencing the child. For example, a child may choose a parent who is especially hurt by the divorce and is emotionally manipulating the child (Hatherley, 1973). Or the child may reject the parent he perceives as responsible for the divorce (Weiss, 1979b). Furthermore, the child who testifies to his own interests risks offending and alienating the parent not chosen. This issue poses a delicate dilemma for the judge who wishes to allow the child an opportunity to exercise his rights but who also realizes that such an expression may inadvertently precipitate family responses and courses of action injurious to the child.

Allowing the child to speak candidly in the judge's chambers protects confidentiality for the child but may violate the parent's rights. These off-the-record discussions may not be a part of the trial records (Weiss, 1979b). These proceedings thus constitute a "secret court" or "back door" to the courtroom, in which justice is not administered openly (Siegel and Hurley, 1977). Our legal system establishes a defendant's right to an open trial in which all information is presented in the courtroom. Because these interviews with the judge are not made public, parents are not able to address the issues and defend themselves. They are, in a sense, tried secretly.

Another aspect of child custody litigation may also infringe on the parent's rights. In our legal system, courts permit as evidence only the information germane to the case; irrelevant material is blocked or struck from the record. In custody litigation, only data relevant to judging the adult's effectiveness as a parent should be presented. "Fault" within the marriage should not enter into this assessment. Although only a few states still officially allow marital fault to be used in the custody hearing, this type of material may enter in as the judge attempts to determine whether a parent is "fit." Information on sexual activity, such as adultery or living together without marriage, may enter into the proceedings even when these behaviors are not related to the parent/child relationship. Mental health professionals still use this type of information in their reports to the court. For example, Chase (1977), a psychiatrist, advocates including information on life-styles in assessing a parent's fitness. He does not indicate which life-style may be most beneficial to the child's development, but since professionals are located in the upper middle class, the preferred life-style probably reflects the norms of that class.

A third area in which parents' rights are challenged is in the postdivorce relationship of the child with the noncustodial parent. What rights does the noncustodial parent have in continuing a relationship with the child? In their response to this issue, Goldstein, Freud, and Solnit (1973) advocated an approach that purportedly protects the child's rights while negating the parent's rights. They state the courts should determine which parent is the "psychological parent," or the one with the better relationship with the child. This parent should be awarded permanent custody; the noncustodial parent will then have no right to visitation or continued contact with the child, unless permitted by the custodial parent. They base their argument on psychoanalytic premises that state the child's needs for a continuous, unbroken relationship with an adult. Unlike adults, children cannot develop positive emotional ties with adults who are unrelated or hostile to each other. Children who try to love adults who are not in a positive relationship with each other become prey to loyalty conflicts (Goldstein, Freud, and Solnit, 1973, pp. 12, 38).

Cutting off rights to visitation and continued contact certainly violates that parent's rights. But critics have argued that this action also denies the child's rights. Several researchers have found that children adapt best to the divorce when they are able to retain relationships with both parents (Hess and Camara, 1979; Wallerstein and Kelly, 1980). Children who are deserted or rejected by the noncustodial parent experience emotional distress and are adversely affected in their development.

Perhaps this last point is key in resolving issues of children's and parents' rights. Any approach that violates the rights of any family member will ultimately have negative consequences for the entire family. Defining these rights as oppositional, requiring a choice for either the adult or child, reflects the adversarial nature of our legal process. If, instead, these rights are perceived as complementary and a compromise is attempted, the family as a whole will benefit.

Certain strategies may be developed to balance the needs of all involved parties. On the first issue—expression of the child's wishes in the court proceedings—interviews in the judge's chambers may be taped and made available to the parents' lawyers. Or the parents may both consent to the private hearing; in the interests of protecting their children from exposure, they may willingly forgo their rights to knowledge of the material.

On the second issue of inclusion of material not germane to assessing the parent's fitness, mental health professionals and attorneys must not be permitted to enter irrelevant information into the record. The judge can stipulate the types of information that he refuses to permit in the courtroom. It is not easy, of course, to know clearly which behaviors are critical to child development and which are extraneous, but too often the traditional mores of professionals, attorneys, and judges have intruded and imposed on the family, when such judgments are clearly not relevant to the issue. When this occurs, children, as well as parents, suffer; the young children have difficulty sustaining healthy relationships with parents who have been labeled by the courts as "bad" (Hatherley, 1973). Focusing on the quality of each parent's relationship with the child has more benefits than assessing fault of the marital partners.

Third, both parents have rights to continued access to their children. Goldstein, Freud, and Solnit based their arguments on the assumption that divorcing parents continue a hostile battle and are not able to cooperate in the interests of the child. Furthermore, they assumed that children are very vulnerable and unable to love two adults who do not love each other. This position overstates the emotional fragility of the child; most children are exposed to marital conflict before the divorce and devise ways to cope with it. Parents can also shield their children from the destructive aspects of the conflict. In the majority of cases, continued contact may be more beneficial than harmful if the child has two psychological parents who both wish to retain their relationship with the child. Visitation should be limited only if it is clearly shown that these contacts are disturbing to the child.

The Politics of Custody Litigation. Custody litigation is difficult because "judges have so much discretion, the decision is so important to those involved, and the task is intrinsically so very difficult" (Weiss, 1979b, p. 330). The high investment of the participants and the ambiguity of the process invite political maneuvering. The "winner" of custody need not necessarily be the more competent parent, but he or she clearly is the one who has been more successful in projecting that image and in gaining community and legal support for this claim. Perhaps the parent who gains custody has been more perceptive than the spouse in defining the situation for exactly what it is—an adversary relationship in which the ex-spouse is no longer a lover but a legal combatant. Strategies are then devised to utilize personal and community resources while minimizing the maneuvers made by the opposing spouse. It may very well be that a masterful command of these resources determines the outcome of this traumatic contest far more than any simple demonstration of "parental competency."

The astute petitioner can, for example, employ a mental

health professional to investigate the family. When professionals are retained by one party, they may have difficulty maintaining an impartial view.

If the first examination does not yield the desired results, the disappointed parent may employ another expert, and a third, if needed. Watson noted that these multiple experts are often used covertly to delay litigation; if one contestant has enough money, this delaying tactic can be continued indefinitely (Watson, 1969, p. 75).

The determined contestant may also obtain the very best legal counsel possible. Again, the partner with the greater resources may be more successful in obtaining an experienced lawyer who can argue more persuasively; perhaps even more important, this lawyer may have a greater knowledge of the politics of the legal system.

Custody litigation also invites political maneuvering between professions; lawyers and mental health professionals have traditionally not trusted each other or cooperated in legal cases (Elkin, 1979; Littner, 1971). The lawyer, for example, may engage the legally uninitiated behavioral scientist in legal gamesmanship and expose inconsistencies in the report. These inconsistencies often reflect the therapist's lack of gamesmanship and not any inherent errors in his or her material (Watson, 1969, p. 76). Conversely, therapists may take matters into their own hands and formulate courses of action without gathering sufficient information or consulting with the attorneys (Ramey, Stender, and Dunn, 1977). Such a contest exposes professional rivalries between the mental health professionals and lawyers; these manipulations of one professional by another do nothing to resolve the family's dilemma.

Custody litigation may never be completely devoid of political manipulation. However, some strategies can be developed to ease tensions and make the process more equitable. Mental health professionals may be retained by the court or by both marital partners. They should work for the family, rather than for one contestant. Lawyers and behavioral scientists may be educated to work together and respect the contribution each has to make to the process. In some areas, such partnerships have been formed and apparently are effective (Postma and Manahan, 1981). The type of partnership may vary from those professionals who consult with each other but work independently to those who work as a team in mediation with the couple. These cooperative efforts diminish professional competition and allow the court to focus more on the family's problems.

In addition, judges can curtail maneuvers that delay procedures. They need not allow repetitive examinations or other tactics that simply impede the process without adding new information.

Conclusions

Emphasis is placed today on the children's rights, and considerable effort is apparently expended on determining their interests, but it may be naive to assume that children's rights are comparable to the parents' (Hatherley, 1973). Ambivalence in the courtroom is demonstrated as judges sometimes express a genuine concern for the child's welfare but at other times act as if children were chattels and custody were a proprietary right of the parents (Hatherley, 1973). Children can exercise only those rights permitted them by adults. They have very little knowledge of the legal process and usually have no access whatsoever to the proceedings. Even if they state a preference, that preference may be overruled if the judge determines other factors are more important. But even more important, no child can force a parent to consider him and keep his interests in mind; he cannot force the parent to behave in ways that are beneficial for his growth and development. Thus, while the rhetoric may focus on the child, adults still retain control of a process that at times may give him very little consideration.

The concerned adult may wonder what approach should be taken with the child when parents divorce. It has been argued that a child needs protection from conflict in a stable, continuous relationship with one adult. It may be unreasonable, however, to assume that children can be shielded from the conflicts and heartbreak of the dissolving marriage. Rather than attempt to ignore or overlook the conflict, parents can help their children learn to cope with it. Through the loving support of adults, children can gain an understanding of both parents. They can be taught to reconcile the differences between parents while not expecting them to agree. They can learn to appreciate different values and be comfortable with different life-styles. The child who learns how to cope with conflict rather than avoid it may, as an adult, have a greater capacity for receiving different ideas and for then formulating his own ideas.

Second, continuity and stability in relationships are desirable, and a child who experiences this condition may be most fortunate. However, few persons, adults or children, can expect to enjoy stability and permanence in an urban society where conflict and change are inherent in everyday living. The citizen in a complex culture must learn to cope with change. Resilience, adaptability, and flexibility befit the child who is to live in this society. A child who is protected from both conflict and change is less well equipped for life in this type of culture.

In the United States today, the concerned parent may discover his most loving gift to his child is not a guarantee of permanence but the realization that love endures change. A loving parent does not need to hang onto the child and insist on constant physical contact. When it is necessary, this parent can show love by letting go and by giving the child an opportunity to develop a relationship with the other parent. This child learns that love transcends distance and time, and real security does not depend on things remaining permanent or constant. The child who learns to cope with conflict and knows that love endures through change can approach life with increased confidence and strength.

Appendix:
Research Notes

𝓥 𝓥

The men and women interviewed in this study were selected from a large random sample of families in an urban county in Northern California. When residents of this county begin the legal process for divorce, they file a petition for dissolution at the courthouse. Cases are numbered sequentially and filed by number. In every fourth section of these files, I selected every divorce case which had been filed between September 1976 and December 1977 and which included children. This procedure yielded an approximately 25 percent sample of all such cases filed during that sixteen-month period.

From these 588 families, I selected men and women for interviews. Early in data collection, I made several decisions on parameters for the sample. I felt time was a critical factor for di-

vorcing couples. Approaching a family too early in the process
was not productive; men and women experiencing stress and
traumatic changes may be reluctant to be involved in a research
study. For some families, resolution of the issue of child custody occurred some time after filing the initial petition for dissolution. Contacting people too long after the separation would,
however, also not be productive. With the passage of time, data
would become more retrospective. Divorced people often move,
making it more difficult to locate a sample. After some deliberation and pretesting, I set the parameters for my sample at six to
eighteen months after filing the initial petition for dissolution.

The second parameter I established was socioeconomic
class. Research has shown that both marital and parenting behaviors are influenced by social class. Working within the limitation
of a small sample of forty families, I decided to control for class
and admit to my sample only families in which the father was
employed as a white-collar worker or professional. For reasons
of accessibility and validity, I used occupation to determine
socioeconomic status. Information on occupations was usually
available in the records, but information on income and education was less often included in the court file. I also felt the data
on occupations were more reliable than data on income. Often
couples fought over money, and I suspect incomes were sometimes underestimated or concealed. Information on occupations
was less subject to this kind of distortion.

I planned to interview an equal number of men and wom-
en in mother- and father-custody families. My final sample
would include ten men and ten women from twenty father-custody families and ten men and ten women from twenty mother-
custody families. Within the 588 families, I located only twenty-
one father-custody cases that were eligible for the interview
sample—that is, the father was a white-collar worker or professional. In four of these twenty-one families, the husband or wife
either had moved from the area or refused to participate. It
was necessary, therefore, to extend the search through additional records to locate three more families to make up the final
total of twenty families.

I had no difficulty locating mother-custody families; 132

families fit the specifications for the interview sample. I interviewed men and women from these families as they emerged in my search. When I had interviewed over ten mother-custody families, I matched my interview sample with families not selected for interview. I chose the remaining families carefully to avoid overrepresentation of any one type of family characteristic. A final comparison of the twenty mother-custody families who participated in the study with the 112 families who were eligible but did not participate indicated they were very similar and did not differ statistically on any important family characteristic, such as age of oldest child, husband's and wife's ages, size of family, or sex of children.

I contacted my chosen subjects through a letter explaining the research study and reassuring them of the confidentiality and voluntary nature of the study. Approximately one week to ten days after the letter, I telephoned them and arranged for an interview.

Ultimately a total of sixty-one families were selected for interviews. Of this number two had reconciled their differences and were not continuing with their plans for divorce. Nineteen of the fifty-nine families were not interviewed either because they could not be located or because they refused to participate (see Table 9). Considering the fifty-nine families eligible for interviews and the forty who responded, the response rate for families was 68 percent. If only the fifty-two families with at

Table 9. Response Rate for Interview Sample.

Families Contacted	59	—	—
Not Available	—	7	—
(Both husband and wife moved from area or could not be located)			
Not Available or Refused	—	7	—
(One partner not available, one partner refused)			
Refused to Participate.	—	5	—
(Both partners refused)			
Interviewed	—	—	40
	59	19	40

Response Rate = 68 percent

least one person still available in the area are considered, the response rate was 77 percent. Keeping in mind the stresses these divorcing families were experiencing, I felt the response rate was quite high.

My major purpose in the interviews was to identify critical events within the family's history, the patterns of responses to these events, and the cumulative consequences of these actions. I included questions on the initiation of the marriage, the arrival of the first and later children, and employment patterns for wife and husband. I also included core areas of marital life for investigation, such as companionship, emotional support, and sexual satisfaction. Finally, since I was assuming that interactions with other persons outside the home may affect marital relationships, I included some questions on support networks.

Having selected the major areas for study, I devised a structured interview schedule. Since I wanted to encourage the respondent to describe and illustrate his or her own experiences, I constructed open-ended questions.

After pretesting the interview schedule with about a dozen persons, I revised it. I omitted sections on early life experiences, as I felt this information was not appropriate to the major thrust of my research, and I enlarged the section on separation and divorce. I included more detailed questions about the legal process, particularly as it involved the issue of child custody.

I included two short questionnaires with my interview schedule. One was an adaptation of Hurvitz's Marital Roles Inventory (Hurvitz, 1960). I revised several of these items and added three new items. The second questionnaire contained thirty items and was an expansion of the scale used by Hobbs (1965; Hobbs and Cole, 1976) to measure the impact of the first child on the marriage. On this latter instrument, potential scores could range from a low of 30, indicating low stress with the birth of the first child, to 150, high stress. Actual range of responses was from 43 to 114, with a mean of 76 and a standard deviation of 17. The standardized item alpha coefficient was .86. The wide range of responses made it an excellent tool for differentiating among respondents, and it had a sufficiently high reliability rating to warrant its use.

In the interviews I followed several strategies to increase consistency and eliminate possible distortion of the data. I structured each interview session carefully to avoid disruptive events and ensure privacy. For example, I avoided times of the day when the children would be present or requiring attention. All interviews were held without a third party present. I assured all respondents of the confidentiality of the material. No one heard the tapes, and only numbers, not names, identified the material. When names were used in the final report or manuscript, they were, of course, pseudonyms. Respondents also knew I was not talking with their lawyer, spouse, or children; none of the material they gave me could be used against them in the legal process.

I attempted to establish rapport with respondents. Before the interview began, I identified myself personally and professionally, taking care not to give them information that might influence the tenor of their responses. I began each interview with more general and less threatening questions and gave the respondent an opportunity to feel at ease before probing into the more sensitive areas of marital life. If respondents appeared to become overwhelmed by the material, I offered them the opportunity to stop the interview and resume it at another time. Four interviews required two sessions. I conducted all interviews myself, thereby eliminating the possibility of inconsistency between interviewers.

All interviews were taped and then typed verbatim. Analysis of data assumed two phases. First, I devised a list of questions that I felt were crucial to understanding each family. I then read through each case and summarized the material, using the questions as a basis for the summary.

Second, I undertook an analysis of family interaction patterns. I divided photocopies of every interview into segments; each segment focused on a specific area of marital life or described a particular family episode. Approximately thirty-five to sixty interview segments were obtained for each of the forty persons in the sample. While some interview segments revealed some aspect of the relationship with children, others highlighted the marital relationship.

In my analysis, I devised measures for both parent/child and husband/wife interaction. I adapted Baumrind's scales to assess parental efficacy and nurturance (Baumrind, 1972). I defined *efficacy* as the parent's potency or power to produce desired results. This measure reflected both the parent's confidence in child rearing and willingness to exercise that power by assuming responsibility for the child. This scale had five categories:

1. Parent relates to child in unsure, insecure fashion. Parent tends to be reactive rather than active. Opposition from child evokes evasion, retreat, or other signs of impotence, or undue harshness.
2. Parent does not regard self as a particularly competent parent and is somewhat shaken by threats to his competency as a parent.
3. Parent feels some ambiguity about the parental role and some doubts as to competence. He may express some beliefs about what he should do but lacks the conviction that he has the potency to perform in that desired way.
4. Parent regards self as a competent parent, remaining quite confident in his relationship with the children. He regards himself as capable of guiding child.
5. Parent relates to children in self-assured, secure manner. Parent is active rather than reactive and initiates interaction with children. He assumes full responsibility for them and feels he is a potent force in their lives. He perceives ways in which he can help children cope with their problems and does not leave their solution to other persons, such as spouse, teachers, kin.

Nurturance included warmth and involvement with the child and also included five categories:

1. Parent's needs generally take precedence, and parent is frequently inaccessible. Parent may know little about his children and expresses little awareness of their special problems or needs. Parent does not enjoy interaction with children

and prefers spending his time outside their company. Children are treated coolly, harshly, and unsympathetically.

2. Parent does his duty and is not negligent, but he really does not enjoy the children's company and treats them coolly. Whenever possible, he may attempt to find ways of avoiding care or taking short-cuts, without too much thought for children's comfort or enjoyment.

3. Parent is accessible and not neglecting but is not always involved. Parent may be physically present but may be inconsistent in supplying children's needs. He may care but not know how to express it or may be too preoccupied with own life.

4. Parent is warm, accessible, and supportive. He has a knowledge of his children and is concerned with their welfare and aware of their problems. He spends time with them and enjoys them.

5. Parent is loving, supportive, responsive, and accessible. He obviously enjoys children's company and conversation. He is aware of their strengths and considers their unique problems. He takes pride in their development.

In analysis of marital behaviors, I examined each interview segment and identified the most basic, fundamental units of behavior. I called these simple units of behavior "gestures" and adopted Turner's definition of *gesture*: "A gesture is any behavior that can be assigned some meaning by the actor or observer" (Turner, 1970, p. 21). In everyday use, a gesture means a movement of the body to express a feeling or attitude; in this study I enlarged that definition to include all verbal and nonverbal behaviors that had meaning for the participants.

As my analysis of interview segments progressed, I discovered these numerous and varied gestures could be categorized into three basic groups: behaviors that moved the husband and wife *away from* each other (Gestures of Avoidance), *toward* each other (Gestures of Appeal), or *against* each other (Gestures of Attack). Gestures of Appeal were further subdivided into *Subordinate* and *Superordinate* Appeal Gestures. As I organized gestures within these categories, I noted they varied greatly in intensity as well as style. Some gestures were very subtle; these "below the surface" behaviors were seldom noticed by either the husband or wife. Subtle gestures were important and contributed to a definition of the marriage.

In my analysis, I noted that with time, the subtle gestures of early marriage became more intense and increased in their visibility. In these forty families, the most clearly defined, highly visible gestures usually appeared immediately before the breakup of the marriage or during the period of separation or divorce. I charted the escalations of behaviors, the changes within the marital relationship, and the events precipitating these changes.

I was eventually able to construct an outline with gestures arranged in varying levels of intensity within each of the four types (Table 10). Using this guide, I compared families and grouped those together that were similar in style, intensity, and evolution of marital patterns. I identified six different patterns of family interaction: Fragile Bond, Fractured Families, Doll's House Marriages, Perfect Model, Stalemate, and Unformed Families (Table 11).

I used the interview segments to place each family in one of the six patterns. However, working with isolated bits of data may distort the whole. Breaking up interviews into segments may destroy the totality of the philosophy expressed by participants. I therefore reread each interview *in toto* to ascertain whether individual families had been placed correctly.

After making final decisions on placement of the families, I examined the families in each pattern to determine the way in which the patterns of behaviors had propelled the family toward separation and divorce. I noted the ways these patterns of family interaction influenced the family's approach to the issue of child custody at the time of separation. Although all parents in each pattern did not have identical responses to the issue of custody, I did perceive many similarities; differences could often be explained by considering other important factors of sex and age of the children, the parent's access to resources outside the marriage, and the value the husband and wife placed on the parenting role.

Table 10. Gestures in Four Modes of Marital Interaction by Levels of Intensity.

Level of Intensity	Mode of Interaction			
	Appeal to Bonding		Avoidance of Bonding	Attack on Bonding
	Subordinate	Superordinate		
Low	Posturing Rewarding	Persuading Rewarding	Labeling Discounting Dismissing Affirming	Passive negation Latent anger
Low to Moderate	Status reduction (of self): Confessing Blaming self Status inflation (of partner): Accommodating	Status reduction (of partner): Trivializing Ridiculing Status inflation (of self): Demanding	Separation and substitution Splitting roles Emotional withholding	Layered criticisms
Moderate	Emotional appeal and display: Crying, pleading		Subtracting	Verbal threats
Moderately High	Depression	Depression	Leaving	Display of violence
High	Mental illness	Threatening violence to self and others (suicide)	Abandonment	Physical assault (murder)

Table 11. Mode and Intensity of Interaction in Six Family Patterns.

Family Pattern	Primary Mode	Secondary Mode	Intensity
Fragile Bond			
Husband	Avoidance	Superordinate	Low to moderate
Wife	Avoidance	Subordinate	Low to moderate
Fractured Families			
Husband	Attack	Avoidance	High
Wife	Subordinate	Avoidance	High
Doll's House			
Husband	Superordinate	Avoidance	Moderate to high
Wife	Avoidance	Subordinate	Low to moderate
Perfect Model			
Husband	Avoidance	Superordinate and attack	Low
Wife	Subordinate	Avoidance	Low
Stalemate			
Husband	Avoidance	—	Moderate
Wife	Avoidance	Subordinate and attack	Moderately high
Unformed			
Husband	Superordinate and subordinate	Attack	Moderately high
Wife	Avoidance	Attack	Moderate to high

I was thus able to construct models of marital process, beginning with the initial stages of marriage, continuing through the childbearing and child-rearing stages to the time of separation and divorce. When divorce behaviors were approached through this family history, the actions taken by both the husband and wife were predictable. Within the context of the marital behaviors, their actions in divorce made sense. Interaction during the divorce period intensified but mirrored to a remarkable degree the interaction patterns of the marriage.

References

🍂 🍂

Ambert, A. "Differences in Children's Behavior Toward Custodial Mothers and Fathers." *Journal of Marriage and the Family,* 1982, *44,* 73-86.

Anthony, E. J. "Children at Risk from Divorce: A Review." In E. J. Anthony and C. Koupernik (Eds.), *The Child in His Family.* Vol. 3: *Children at Psychiatric Risk.* New York: Wiley, 1974.

Baumrind, D. *Parent Rating Scales.* Berkeley, Calif.: Institute of Human Development, 1972.

Beal, E. W. "Children of Divorce: A Family Systems Perspective." *Journal of Social Issues,* 1979, *35,* 140-154.

Benedek, E. P., and Benedek, R. S. "New Child Custody Laws: Making Them Do What They Say." *American Journal of Orthopsychiatry,* 1972, *42,* 825-834.

217

Benedek, R. S., and Benedek, E. P. "Children of Divorce: Can We Meet Their Needs?" *Journal of Social Issues,* 1979, *35,* 155-169.

Berger, P. L., and Kellner, H. "Marriage and the Construction of Reality." In H. Robboy, S. Greenblatt, and C. Clark (Eds.), *Social Interaction: Introductory Readings in Sociology.* New York: St. Martin's Press, 1979.

Berkove, G. F. "Perceptions of Husband Support by Returning Women Students." *Family Coordinator,* 1979, *28,* 451-457.

Black, H. C. *Black's Law Dictionary.* (4th ed.) St. Paul, Minn.: West Publishing, 1951.

Blood, R. O., and Wolfe, D. M. *Husbands and Wives: The Dynamics of Married Living.* New York: Free Press, 1960.

Bodenheimer, B. M. "Progress Under the Uniform Child Custody Jurisdiction Act and Remaining Problems: Punitive Decrees, Joint Custody and Excessive Modifications." *California Law Review,* 1977, *65,* 978-1014.

Booth, A. "Does Wives' Employment Cause Stress for Husbands?" *Family Coordinator,* 1979, *28,* 445-449.

Bortner, R. W., Bohn, C. J., and Hultsch, D. F. "A Cross-Cultural Study of the Effects of Children on Parental Assessment of Past, Present and Future." *Journal of Marriage and the Family,* 1974, *36,* 370-378.

Brown, B. A., Freedman, A. E., Katz, H. N., and Price, A. M. *Women's Rights and the Law.* New York: Praeger, 1977.

Brown, R. C. "Comment: Custody of Children." *Indiana Law Journal,* 1927, *2,* 325-330.

Burke, R. J., and Weir, T. "Relationship of Wives' Employment Status to Husband, Wife and Pair Satisfaction and Performance." *Journal of Marriage and the Family,* 1976, *38,* 279-287.

Burr, W. R. "Satisfaction with Various Aspects of Marriage over the Life Cycle: A Random Middle Class Sample." *Journal of Marriage and the Family,* 1970, *32,* 29-37.

Cantor, I., and Ferguson, P. L. "Family Counseling in the Conciliation Court: An Alternative to Custody Litigation." *Conciliation Courts Review,* 1976, *14,* 1-8.

Chase, G. "Criteria for Psychiatric Evaluations in Child Custody Contests." *Conciliation Courts Review,* 1977, *15,* 19-27.

Coogler, O. J. *Structured Mediation in Divorce Settlement.* Lexington, Mass.: Heath, 1978.

Cromwell, R. E., and Olson, D. H. *Power in Families.* New York: Wiley, 1975.

David, D. S., and Brannon, R. (Eds.). *The Forty-Nine Percent Majority: The Male Sex Role.* Menlo Park, Calif.: Addison-Wesley, 1976.

DeFrain, J., and Eirick, R. "Coping as Divorced Single Parents: A Comparative Study of Fathers and Mothers." *Family Relations,* 1981, *30,* 265-273.

Dyer, E. D. "Parenthood as Crisis: A Re-Study." *Marriage and Family Living,* 1963, *25,* 196-201.

Elkin, M. "Interprofessional Cooperation Between the Law and the Behavioral Sciences: A Priority Need." *Conciliation Courts Review,* 1979, *17,* iii-vi.

Ellsworth, P., and Levy, R. "Legislative Reform of Child Custody Adjudication." *Law and Society Review,* 1969, *4,* 166-233.

Fain, H. M. "The Role and Responsibility of the Lawyer in Custody Cases." *Family Law Quarterly,* 1967, *1,* 36-47.

Farrell, W. *The Liberated Man.* New York: Random House, 1974.

Fasteau, M. F. *The Male Machine.* New York: McGraw-Hill, 1974.

Folberg, H. J., and Graham, M. "Joint Custody of Children Following Divorce." *University of California Davis Law Review,* 1979, *12,* 523-581.

Foster, H. H., and Freed, D. J. "Child Custody." *New York University Law Review,* 1964, *39.* Part I: 423-443. Part II: 615-630.

Freed, D. J., and Foster, H. H. "Taking Out the Fault but Not the Sting." *Trial,* 1976, *12,* 10-12, 19.

Gaddis, S. M. "Divorce Decision Making: Alternatives to Litigation." *Conciliation Courts Review,* 1978, *16,* 43-45.

Gasser, R. D., and Taylor, C. M. "Role Adjustments of Single Parent Fathers with Dependent Children." *Family Coordinator,* 1976, *25,* 397-401.

George, V., and Wilding, P. *Motherless Families.* London: Routledge & Kegan Paul, 1972.

Glenn, N., and McLanahan, S. "Children and Marital Happiness: A Further Specification of the Relationship." *Journal of Marriage and the Family*, 1982, *44*, 63-72.

Glenn, N., and Weaver, C. "A Multivariate Multisurvey Study of Marital Happiness." *Journal of Marriage and the Family*, 1978, *40*, 269-282.

Glick, P. C. "Children of Divorced Parents in Demographic Perspective." *Journal of Social Issues*, 1979, *35*, 170-182.

Goldstein, J., Freud, A., and Solnit, A. J. *Beyond the Best Interest of the Child*. New York: Free Press, 1973.

Hansen, R. W. "Guardians Ad Litem in Divorce and Custody Cases: Protection of the Child's Interests." *Journal of Family Law*, 1964, *4*, 181-184.

Harris, M. W. "The Child as Hostage." In I. R. Stuart and L. E. Abt (Eds.), *Children of Separation and Divorce*. New York: Grossman, 1972.

Hatherley, J. E. "The Role of the Child's Wishes in California Custody Proceedings." *University of California Davis Law Review*, 1973, *6*, 332-353.

Haynes, J. N. "Managing Conflict: The Role of the Mediator." *Conciliation Courts Review*, 1980, *18*, 9-13.

Hess, R. D., and Camara, K. A. "Post-Divorce Family Relationships as Mediating Factors in the Consequences of Divorce for Children." *Journal of Social Issues*, 1979, *35*, 79-96.

Hetherington, E. M., Cox, M., and Cox, R. "Play and Social Interaction in Children Following Divorce." *Journal of Social Issues*, 1979a, *35*, 26-47.

Hetherington, E. M., Cox, M., and Cox, R. "Stress and Coping in Divorce: A Focus on Women." In J. E. Gullahorn (Ed.), *Psychology and Women: In Transition*. New York: Wiley, 1979b.

Hobbs, D. F., Jr. "Parenthood as Crisis: A Third Study." *Journal of Marriage and the Family*, 1965, *27*, 367-372.

Hobbs, D. F., Jr., and Cole, S. P. "Transition to Parenthood: A Decade Replication." *Journal of Marriage and the Family*, 1976, *38*, 725-731.

Hochschild, A. "Emotion Work, Feeling Rules and Social Structure." *American Journal of Sociology*, 1979, *85*, 551-575.

Holmstrom, L. *The Two-Career Family.* Cambridge, Mass.: Schenkman, 1972.

Holy, M. C. "Guidelines for Guardians Ad Litem—Custody Disputes." *Conciliation Courts Review,* 1977, *15,* 13-15.

Hooper, J. O. "My Wife, the Student." *Family Coordinator,* 1979, *28,* 459-464.

Huber, J., and Spitze, G. "Considering Divorce: An Expansion of Becker's Theory of Marital Instability." *American Journal of Sociology,* 1980, *86,* 75-89.

Hurvitz, N. "The Marital Roles Inventory and the Measurement of Marital Adjustment." *Journal of Clinical Psychology,* 1960, *16,* 377-380.

Ibsen, H. *A Doll's House.* (W. Archer, Trans.) Boston: Walter H. Baker, n.d.

Inker, M. L., and Perretta, C. A. "A Child's Right to Counsel in Custody Cases." *Family Law Quarterly,* 1971, *5,* 108-120.

Jacobs, A. C., and Goebel, J. *Cases on Domestic Relations.* Brooklyn, N.Y.: Foundation Press, 1962.

Katz, A. J. "Lone Fathers: Perspectives and Implications for Family Policy." *Family Coordinator,* 1979, *28,* 521-528.

Kemper, T. D. *A Social Interactional Theory of Emotions.* New York: Wiley, 1978.

Kram, S. W., and Frank, N. "The Future of 'Tender' Years." *Trial,* 1976, *12,* 14-15.

Kressel, K., Lopez-Morillas, M., Weinglass, J., and Deutsch, M. "Professional Intervention in Divorce: The Views of Lawyers, Psychotherapists and Clergy." In G. Levinger and O. C. Moles (Eds.), *Divorce and Separation.* New York: Basic Books, 1979.

LeMasters, E. E. "Parenthood as Crisis." *Marriage and Family Living,* 1957, *19,* 352-355.

Levinger, G., and Moles, O. C. (Eds.). *Divorce and Separation.* New York: Basic Books, 1979.

Little, M. "Family Processes in the Determination of Child Custody." Unpublished doctoral dissertation, Department of Sociology, University of California at Berkeley, 1980.

Little, M. "Financial Dislocations Among Divorcing Families." Paper presented at American Sociological Association meeting, San Francisco, September 1982.

222   References

Littner, N. "The Doctor's Role in Contested Child Custody
    Matters." *Conciliation Courts Review*, 1971, *9*, 34-36.

McDermott, J. J., Jr. "Divorce and Its Psychiatric Sequelae in
    Children." *Archives of General Psychiatry*, 1970, *23*, 421-
    427.

Madden, J. W. *Handbook of the Law of Persons and Domestic
    Relations.* St. Paul, Minn.: West Publishing Co., 1931.

Meissner, M., Humphreys, E., Meis, S., and Scheu, W. "No Exit
    for Wives: Sexual Division of Labor and the Cumulation of
    Household Demands." *Canadian Review of Sociology and
    Anthropology*, 1975, *12*, 424-439.

Mendes, H. A. "Single Fathers." *Family Coordinator*, 1976,
    25, 439-444.

Mendes, H. A. "How Divorced Fathers Obtain Custody: A Re-
    view of Research." *Conciliation Courts Review*, 1979, *17*, 27-
    30.

Miller, B. C. "A Multivariate Developmental Model of Marital
    Satisfaction." *Journal of Marriage and the Family*, 1976, *38*,
    643-657.

Miller, B. C., and Sollie, D. L. "Normal Stresses During the
    Transition to Parenthood." *Family Relations*, 1980, *29*, 459-
    465.

Miller, D. "Joint Custody." *Family Law Quarterly*, 1979, *13*,
    345-412.

Milmed, P. K. "Due Process for Children: A Right to Counsel in
    Custody Proceedings." *New York University Review of Law
    and Social Change*, 1974, *4*, 177-189.

Mnookin, R. H. "Child-Custody Adjudication: Judicial Func-
    tions in the Face of Indeterminacy." *Law and Contemporary
    Problems*, 1975, *39*, 226-293.

"Notes: Reciprocity of Rights and Duties Between Parent and
    Child." *Harvard Law Review*, 1928, *42*, 112-115.

Nye, F. I. "Effects on Mother." In L. W. Hoffman and F. I.
    Nye, *Working Mothers: An Evaluative Review of the Conse-
    quences for Wife, Husband, and Child.* San Francisco: Jossey-
    Bass, 1974.

O'Brien, M. "Becoming a Lone Father: A New Male Response
    to Divorce?" In *Proceedings* from Nineteenth International

Committee on Family Research, Seminar on Divorce and Remarriage, Leuven, Belgium, August 1981.

Okpaku, S. R. "Psychology: Impediment or Aid in Child Custody Cases?" *Rutgers Law Review,* 1976, *29,* 1117-1153.

Orthner, D. K., Brown, T., and Ferguson, D. "Single-Parent Fatherhood: An Emerging Family Lifestyle." *Family Coordinator,* 1976, *25,* 429-437.

Orthner, D. K., and Lewis, K. "Evidence of Single-Father Competence in Childrearing." *Family Law Quarterly,* 1979, *13,* 27-47.

Paloma, M. M., and Garland, T. N. "The Married Professional Woman: A Study in the Tolerance of Domestication." *Journal of Marriage and the Family,* 1971, *33,* 531-540.

Pleck, J. H., and Sawyer, J. *Men and Masculinity.* Englewood Cliffs, N.J.: Prentice-Hall, 1974.

Pohlman, E. H. *Psychology of Birth Planning.* Cambridge, Mass.: Schenkman, 1969.

Postma, S., and Manahan, J. H. "A Lawyer-Therapist Team's Strategy for the Process of Divorce: A Working Model and Its Implications for Research." Paper presented at Nineteenth International Committee on Family Research, Seminar on Divorce and Remarriage, Leuven, Belgium, August 1981.

Ramey, M. L., Stender, F., and Dunn, G. "Report of the California Women Lawyers, Child Custody Project." Unpublished manuscript, San Francisco, 1977.

Rapoport, R., and Rapoport, R. N. "The Dual Career Family." *Human Relations,* 1969, *22,* 3-30.

Rapoport, R., and Rapoport, R. N. *Dual Career Families Reexamined: New Integrations of Work and Family.* New York: Harper & Row, 1976.

Raven, B., Centers, R., and Rodrigues, A. "The Bases of Conjugal Power." In R. E. Cromwell and D. H. Olson (Eds.), *Power in Families.* New York: Wiley, 1975.

Renee, K. S. "Correlates of Dissatisfaction in Marriage." *Journal of Marriage and the Family,* 1970, *32,* 54-67.

Robbins, N. N. "Legal Standards for Determining 'Best Interests of the Child.'" *Family Coordinator,* 1974, *23,* 87-90.

Roberts, A. R., and Roberts, B. J. "Divorce and the Child: A

Pyrrhic Victory?" In A. R. Roberts (Ed.), *Childhood Deprivation*. Springfield, Ill.: Thomas, 1974.

Rollins, B. C., and Cannon, K. L. "Marital Satisfaction over the Family Life Cycle: A Reevaluation." *Journal of Marriage and the Family*, 1974, *36*, 271-283.

Rollins, B. C., and Feldman, H. "Marital Satisfaction over the Family Life Cycle." *Journal of Marriage and the Family*, 1970, *32*, 20-27.

Roman, M., and Haddad, W. *The Disposable Parent: The Case for Joint Custody*. New York: Holt, Rinehart and Winston, 1978.

Rossi, A. "Transition to Parenthood." *Journal of Marriage and the Family*, 1968, *30*, 26-39.

Russell, C. S. "Transition to Parenthood: Problems and Gratifications." *Journal of Marriage and the Family*, 1974, *36*, 294-301.

Santrock, J. W., and Warshak, R. A. "Father Custody and Social Development in Boys and Girls." *Journal of Social Issues*, 1979, *35*, 112-125.

Scanzoni, J. "Strategies for Changing Male Family Roles: Research and Practice Implications." *Family Coordinator*, 1979, *28*, 435-442.

Schouler, J., and Blakemore, A. *Marriage, Divorce, Separation and Domestic Relations* (Vol. 1). (6th ed.) Albany, N.Y.: Matthew Bender, 1921.

Sheffner, D. J., and Suarez, J. M. "The Postdivorce Clinic." *American Journal of Psychiatry*, 1975, *132*, 442-444.

Shepherd, R. E., Jr. "Solomon's Sword: Adjudication of Child Custody." *University of Richmond Law Review*, 1974, *8*, 151-200.

Siegel, D. M., and Hurley, S. "The Role of the Child's Preference in Custody Proceedings." *Family Law Quarterly*, 1977, *11*, 1-58.

Smith, R. M., and Smith, C. W. "Child Rearing and Single-Parent Fathers." *Family Relations*, 1981, *30*, 411-417.

Spanier, G. B., and Lewis, R. S. "Marital Quality: A Review of the Seventies." *Journal of Marriage and the Family*, 1980, *42*, 825-839.

Spitze, G. D., and Waite, L. J. "Wives' Employment: The Role of Husbands' Perceived Attitudes." *Journal of Marriage and the Family*, 1981, *43*, 117-124.

Staines, G. L., Pleck, J., Shepard, L. J., and O'Connor, P. "Wives' Employment Status and Marital Adjustment: Yet Another Look." *Psychology of Women Quarterly*, 1978, *3*, 90-120.

Steinzor, B. *When Parents Divorce.* New York: Pantheon, 1969.

Taylor, A. Y. "Toward a Comprehensive Theory of Mediation." *Conciliation Courts Review*, 1981, *19*, 1-12.

Tooley, K. "Antisocial Behavior and Social Alienation, Post Divorce: The 'Man of the House' and His Mother." *American Journal of Orthopsychiatry*, 1976, *46*, 33-42.

Toomin, M. K. "Understanding the Child of Divorce." In R. E. Hardy and J. G. Cull (Eds.), *Creative Divorce Through Social and Psychological Approaches.* Springfield, Ill.: Thomas, 1974.

Tritico, L. "Notes: Child Custody: Preference to the Mother." *Louisiana Law Review*, 1974, *34*, 881-889.

Turner, R. *Family Interaction.* New York: Wiley, 1970.

Waldron, H., and Routh, D. K. "The Effect of the First Child on the Marital Relationship." *Journal of Marriage and the Family*, 1981, *43*, 785-788.

Walker, K. E., and Woods, M. E. *Time Use: A Measure of Household Production of Family Goods and Services.* Washington, D.C.: American Home Economics Association, 1976.

Wallerstein, J. S., and Kelly, J. B. *Surviving the Break-up: How Children and Parents Cope with Divorce.* New York: Basic Books, 1980.

Watson, A. W. "The Children of Armageddon: Problems of Custody Following Divorce." *Syracuse Law Review*, 1969, *21*, 55-86.

Watson, M. A. "Custody Alternatives: Defining the Best Interests of the Children." *Family Relations*, 1981, *30*, 474-479.

Weiss, R. S. *Deciding the Custody of Children of Separating Parents: A Preliminary Literature Review.* Springfield, Va.: National Technical Information Service, 1976.

Weiss, R. S. "Growing Up a Little Faster: The Experience of

Growing Up in a Single-Parent Household." *Journal of Social Issues,* 1979a, *35,* 97-111.

Weiss, R. S. "Issues in the Adjudication of Custody When Parents Separate." In G. Levinger and O. C. Moles (Eds.), *Divorce and Separation.* New York: Basic Books, 1979b.

Westman, J. C., and Cline, D. W. "Role of Child Psychiatry in Divorce." *Archives of General Psychiatry,* 1970, *23,* 416-420.

Yogev, S. "Do Professional Women Have Egalitarian Marital Relationships?" *Journal of Marriage and the Family,* 1981, *43,* 865-871.

Young, M., and Willmott, P. *The Symmetrical Family.* New York: Pantheon, 1974.

Index

𝒱 𝒱

A

Adultery: as criterion for unfitness, 8-9; and employment, 28; in Fractured Family, 68-69; in Perfect Model Marriage, 104-106, 110-111; in Stalemate Marriage, 93-94

Alcoholism and drug addiction: as criterion for unfitness, 9; in Fractured Families, 12, 59, 67-69, 71; and Uncommitted Parenting, 130

Ambert, A., 183-184

American Bar Association, 9

Anger: in Fractured Families, 58-59, 64-67; latent, 61-62; in Split Parenting, 144-145; in Stalemate Marriage, 93-94

Anthony, E. J., 164, 166, 189

Appeal behaviors. *See* Subordinate behaviors; Superordinate behaviors

Arbitration, 197

Attack behaviors: concept of, 11-12; in Fractured Families, 58-67; gestures indicating, 213-216; in Perfect Model Marriages, 101-105; in Stalemate Marriages, 93-94

Avoidance behaviors: concept of, 11-13; in Fractured Families, 58-64, 68-69; in Fragile Bond Marriages, 46-56; gestures indicating, 213-216; in Perfect Model Marriages, 98-101; in Stalemate Marriages, 89-94; in Unformed Families, 112-114

227

forming of rules and definitions by, 150-160; impact of, on children, 160-166; rules about, 150-153; shift in, 84-89, 158, 163; shifts in, and child's experience, 160-167; status and love related to, 153-157

Powering, definition of, 3-4

Pregnancy: impact of, 37-40; stress in, 122, 128

Price, A. M., 1, 10

R

Ramey, M. L., 204

Rapoport, R., 176, 178, 180

Rapoport, R. N., 176, 178, 180

Raven, B., 157

Reciprocity, principle of, 5-7

Renee, K. S., 174

Rewarding behavior, 78-79

Robbins, N. N., 193

Roberts, A. R., 189, 193

Roberts, B. J., 189, 193

Rodrigues, A., 157

Rollins, B. C., 173-174

Roman, M., 190

Rome, custody in, 4-5

Ross v. *Richardson*, 6

Rossi, A., 173

Routh, D. K., 174

Russell, C. S., 173

S

Sampling techniques, 10-11, 207-210

Santrock, J. W., 185

Sawyer, J., 181

Scanzoni, J., 179-181

Scheu, W., 175

Schouler, J., 5-6

Separating and substituting behavior, 49-53

Services of children, 6-7

Sexual relationship, 33-35, 113

Shared Parenting: and child as stabilizer, 121-124; concept of, 14, 118-121

Sheffner, D. J., 193

Shelley v. *Westbrooke*, 8

Shepard, L. J., 176-178

Shepherd, R. E., 9, 192-193, 198

Siegel, D. M., 199-200

Size of families: in Doll's House Marriage, 77; in Fragile Bond Marriage, 46-47; in Perfect Model Marriage, 98; and Shared Parenting, 122; and Uncommitted Parenting, 129

Smith, C. W., 184

Smith, R. M., 184

Social class, 10-11, 208

Sollie, D. L., 174

Solnit, A. J., 201-203

Spanier, G. B., 173-174

Spitze, G. D., 180

Split Parenting: and child as caretaker, 139-146; concept of, 14-15, 118-122; custody in, 145

Stabilizer, child as: concept of, 14-15, 119-121; in Paternal Parenting, 131; in Shared Parenting, 121-125; in Split Parenting, 140, 146

Staines, G. L., 176-178

Stalemate marriages: concept of, 13, 16; custody in, 95; and Doll's House Marriage, 74; and Fragile Bond Marriage, 46-47; interactions in, 216; and Paternal Parenting, 131; withholding and withdrawing in, 92-95; and women's needs and rights, 89-95

Status: emotional response to loss of, 155-157; loss of, sex differences in, 154-155; of partners in marriage, 153-154; reduction and inflation of, 80-84; shifts in, and child's experience, 160-167; women's loss of, in Fractured Families, 59-64, 70

Steinzor, B., 162, 182

Stender, F., 204

Suarez, J. M., 193

Subordinate behaviors: concept of, 11-12; in Doll's House Marriages, 76-85; in Fractured Families, 58-